The Song of God

An American Interpretation of the Bhagavad Gita

By John Gilbert

The Song of God: An American Interpretation of the
Bhagavad Gita

By John Gilbert

First Edition

Published in the United States by John Gilbert

ISBN: 9798846708969

Cover artwork is in the public domain

Other books by John Gilbert:

    Pseudo-Hermetica for the 21st Century: A
    Modern Mystical Philosophy using Ancient
    Literary Forms

Unless otherwise stated, whenever the masculine gender is used, both men and women are included.

Preface

There is something rather than nothing. This is Cosmos.

A human may only glimpse a fragment of this Cosmos. This is Aesthesis.

Some are aware that Aesthesis exists, and others are not. This is Gnosis.

God rode into battle in an Abrams tank on the night of February 20, 1991. He had been hand-selected to drive the lead tank of a four-tank platoon by First Lieutenant Arthur James Nash. They had been friends since basic training at the U.S. Armor School at Fort Knox, Kentucky. From there, A.J. Nash went off to Officer Candidate School, but still kept in touch with his trusted confidant, who was using the name of Sergeant Christopher Josephson in this world.

When A.J. arrived in the desert months before, he happened to run into SGT Josephson at one of those giant tent chow halls the Army is so fond of. Both of them set out to do some catching-up over lunch, finding out in the process that they had both been assigned to the same outfit. Later, when A.J. was given the mission to take his platoon on a recon-in-force against the Iraqis, he knew exactly who he wanted for a driver. He had a wide selection of motivated, well-trained, and eager tankers at his disposal. But, it was really no choice- SGT Josephson had something special about him, a calming effect maybe, that A.J. needed on his side. He trusted SGT Josephson entirely, though he couldn't satisfactorily explain to himself why that was the case. It might have been that SGT Josephson's advice was never wrong, and it helped A.J. stay out of trouble on many occasions during basic. Regardless, it would be A.J.'s friend driving for him on the night of his first combat action- it was the right choice.

An M1A1 tank whines and purrs through the headphones of the crew's CVC (Combat Vehicle Crewman) helmets. Inside, under the dim red interior lamps, there is a smell unique to the Abrams- a sort of oily, paint and metal with a touch of diesel smell. It's not repugnant, but rather comforting to the tanker. Perhaps it reminds them of the feeling of invincibility they first felt inside all that armor. It's easy to get a God complex when you are fast, bullet-proof, and can literally destroy anything you set your eyes upon. The Abrams was the finest chariot on the battlefield. A.J. didn't suffer from a God complex that night, though. He suffered from the human condition.

A.J.'s Sorrow

From the tank commander's position in the turret, A.J. strained with one eye through the sight in front of him. Through it, he had a green-illuminated view of the night desert. It saw whatever the gunner was looking at, and could detect heat sources miles away. While the thermal sights were working fine, there had been problems with the crew's communication system all night. The problem might have been in the CVC helmets or the "spaghetti cables" that connected them to the commo boxes. The problem might have been in the commo boxes themselves, but A.J. had been unable to fix it on the move. It was no big deal to him, because he still had communication with SGT Josephson, whose position in the driver's hole was isolated from the other three men in the turret. A.J. could still communicate with the gunner and loader in the turret by gesturing or just plain yelling over the noise of the tank. Now, he used his foot to tap the gunner on the shoulder.

A.J. saw the "hot spots" first, far in the distance. "Go to ten power!" A.J. shouted, while making the sliding gesture with his hand that indicated that the gunner should increase the magnification of the thermal sights.

With that, the green picture in A.J.'s sight narrowed but increased in magnification. He grabbed the joystick control that took over the movement of the gun and turret from the gunner and searched for the distant hot spots he had seen a moment before. He couldn't find them immediately in the undulating surface of the night desert, but he did see what looked like a large ripple in the sand about one hundred meters in front of them. There, he thought, they might get a good view while staying out of sight themselves.

"Chris," A.J. said into his helmet microphone, "do you see that berm up there, about a hundred in front? Take us to a hull-down position over there." A.J. radioed his intent to the other tanks in his platoon, and to the company commander. A.J. was now the lead tank in the entire formation. He was rolling to a position halfway between the Coalition lines and the Iraqi defenses. SGT Josephson crept up the backside of the berm and brought the tank to a halt, allowing only the gun tube and the sights to stick up from behind the sand dune. A.J. found what he was looking for in only a few seconds. Miles away were the heat signatures of dozens of Iraqi vehicles, appearing as small bright green dots on the horizon. They were exactly where he had expected them to be from the mission briefings. They were exactly in the numbers he expected to find them, too. He did not expect what else he saw through his sights, though.

What he saw were other human beings, just like him. They were fathers, brothers and sons- people who made love, read books, and tucked their own kids in at night. He thought about his own men, too- his tank crew, his platoon, and all the thousands of men and women in the Coalition Forces. Most of them were barely in their 20's. "How can we murder each other?" A.J. thought to himself. "Certainly, the Iraqi dictator is an evil man, but what is the logic in this? Why butchery and mechanized death- people burned and dismembered by fellow human beings?" It was not a wave of guilt that surged over A.J., but a true compassion for others. He didn't lack courage, either, but rather lacked the kind of hatred it takes to murder someone. Suddenly, he felt weak in the limbs and swallowed hard against his parched throat. He was losing the desire to fight, and it caused him to question his duty, his career, and his place in the world.

A.J. needed advice, or at least someone to listen. That is exactly why SGT Josephson was there. Knowing the other crewmen couldn't hear him, he cupped his mic and whispered down to Chris in the driver's hole.

"Chris," he said and swallowed again, "just listen, man. What are we doing? I mean, what good can come out of this? How can anything be the same after this war? All I feel is that if I kill these people, I have sinned and I am evil. A murderer! How can I justify this? Doesn't it just make us as bad as them? Is this my duty, to murder strangers who I have nothing against? Is this what being an officer is all about: I murder some people and I get a promotion and maybe a medal or a raise out of the deal? Those guys over there are prepared to kill us because they believe in what they are doing, too. Who is right? Aren't we the invaders? What do I want with oil and power, or rank, or glory if I have to sell my soul to do it?"

"Bro," he went on almost without a breath, "I know they would kill me given half a chance, but they don't know better. Those guys have been filled with Saddam's lies about us and they probably think we really are the devil. But I know better. I know they are just people doing their jobs- maybe even under threat to their families. Doesn't that make our sin greater? Because I volunteered for the Army, doesn't that make me worse? They see no sin in what they do. Perhaps it is even a 'holy' war for them, but for us we know the evil of war. It degrades the victims and damns the victor. It destroys lives of the innocent, shatters families, disfigures the body. What the hell was I thinking signing up to go to war? It goes against everything I was taught growing up. This war seems a disgrace to all of those patriots who came before, who struggled against oppression and invasion- fought against the Nazis and their death camps. Am I just a high-paid mercenary? Am I so greedy for greatness and money? I would rather die here than take part in murder. Leave me for the enemy- I won't fight them."

With those words, A.J.'s hand slipped away from the control, and the gun-sight slowly drifted off of the hot spots in the distance. He slumped back into his seat, rested his head against the back of the turret, and wondered what to do next. He resolved not to fight, and he would resign his commission as soon as he could. He

would take any dishonor that would come his way, so
long as he could avoid what he considered eternal
damnation for murder.

The Path of Knowledge

As A.J. turned his options over and over in his worried mind, a gentle but firm voice came through his CVC's speakers. "You might have thought about this a long time ago," SGT Josephson said. "I mean, you've had years of training for war. You knew exactly what you were getting into. You aren't here for the college money or any of that crap. You knew you were coming here to fight, and fighting means killing. This is the path you made- and you made it for a reason. You are a warrior and this is your path to fulfillment. You, who is always looking for more inner-knowledge, more awareness, chose this path to see the face of battle. You wanted to experience all facets of your true being. You wanted to know the limits of your potential. Now, here you are, and you want to avoid the knowledge? This is a far worse cowardice than to fear your enemy or death. At least that is a primal fear you were born with. But this has no excuse. It's beneath you. Shake it off! Stand up!"

This shook A.J., but he was stubborn and determined to defend his position. "Iraq is an ancient country, thousands of years old," he said, "These people are noble and worthy of reverence. They have had a great civilization that is many times older than ours. How can I roll through their homes and their cities? How can I ever enjoy anything after being the instrument of destruction in this ancient land? This place was the 'cradle of civilization' and I'm here to crush it. I would rather be on the streets as a bum than to have that on my conscience the rest of my life. Which is worse, winning or losing the war? If we kill them, will we even want to live?" A.J. paused for a moment, considering his own words. "Is this cowardice I feel," A.J. thought out loud, "or real compassion? Am I just fooling myself?" He felt more confused than ever, now unsure of his own feelings and of his own words. "Chris," he almost begged, "I know you. You've never been wrong about this stuff. Tell me what to do. Don't bullshit me, either, just shoot straight. I trust you, man, but I think I'm losin' it right now. Help me pull it together. So help me God, I will not fight."

"A.J.," Chris began again, "you aren't wrong about what you feel. It shows a lot of maturity. You are sad for no reason at all, but you just don't realize it."

A.J. was halted in mid-grief. "What do you mean by that?" he said.

"I mean," Chris continued, "that the truly wise man mourns neither for the dead nor for the living."

A.J. was confused by this remark, but he trusted it was leading somewhere. SGT Josephson began to explain to A.J. what this meant, and why it was true. He said, "There was never a time when God did not exist, or the divine part of you, or me, or any of those Iraqis, and there is not any future in which these things, being God's creation, will ever cease to be.

"Just as you were born with an immortal soul, and that soul remains constant and undamaged throughout your life no matter what, so too does it continue after death. The wise know this.

"Look around you now. These feelings of hot desert sand, cold night wind, pleasure, pain- all of them are caused only by your limited senses taking in all these things. These feelings, like everything, come and go. Nothing is permanent to them. You just have to accept that the world you see and know is only a passing moment, regardless of what you do.

"A calm, rational man accepts pleasure and pain with a balanced mind, and realizes that they are only fleeting feelings, not affecting his unchanging soul. The gates of heaven are open to such a man.

"I'm going to tell you something now that will sound like a riddle, but you will come to see what I mean. When considering the two worlds- the one of fleeting senses, and the one of God's eternal creation, know this: That which does not exist can never come into existence, and that which exists already can never perish, but shall have everlasting life. When you understand this, it will be evidence that you have glimpsed the innermost reality of the universe.

"The Word of God, the all-pervasive divine spirit which IS the universe, is indestructible. It is absurd to think that we, men, have the power to create or destroy anything of God's doing, or to think that we are ever outside of His plan.

"We mortal men say that our bodies die. But that which we call our soul, that divine master of our bodies, is eternal. It cannot be destroyed by other men. So, fight.

"Some look around the battlefield and see people who they call 'killers' and then some see others who they call 'killed'. Those people are ignorant. What do they know of the soul? How can one soul slay another soul?

"Know the soul of a man to have existed before his birth, and to exist after his death, without end, and without change: itself never having been born and not looking forward to a death, ever. How can the mere death of the body somehow cause the destruction of that which God has created?

"Having been told once and for all that the inner reality of the Universe is birthless, deathless, and changeless forever, you no longer can imagine that you are a destroyer. You simply don't have that power.

"Just like you take off an old uniform after it has worn out, so too does the absolute reality which is within us. Death is just a change of clothes, and new people will be born with new faces, like new clothes. Nothing really is destroyed.

"No Iraqi bullet can hit your soul, and no enemy shell can shatter the true reality of creation. Within you and outside of you- us, the tank, the enemy, the sand, the night - everywhere and always is the Nature of God, eternal and changeless forever.

"As humans, we become easily upset at what we cannot see or ponder easily in our minds. We cannot see with our eyes the absolute reality of the world, or fully grasp the idea of this absolute reality within our own beings, because doing so would only leave us with an altered version of it in our heads. Since I've just told you that it is really impossible to know this reality in the usual way, don't worry about trying.

"Let's just say for the sake of argument that you cannot grasp this idea of the absolute immortality of the soul. So what, then? Everyone who is born will certainly die according to every natural and good law of the universe. New souls will come into the world, too. Why should you grieve the inevitable?

"Have you ever thought about where you were before you were born? It didn't seem bad, did it? So, we cannot see beings before they are born into this world. Somewhere between birth and death, we can see them. At death, well, we simply cannot see them again. That bothers us as humans, but what is there in all this to be upset about?

"Let me tell you about that riddle I told you earlier. Absolute reality is not something that is either known by someone or not-known. It is experienced by degrees of insight. Specifically, there are four degrees. First, some people have gazed upon the altar of reality and understood it in all of its wonder. Second, some intuitively know it exists, but can only say that it is wonderful beyond their ability to understand. Next, others know it to be wonderful because someone has told them about it. Finally, there are those who are told about it and have no idea what they are hearing.

"My point is that the absolute reality within each person is indestructible, so there is no reason to ever mourn for anybody.

"So, you should consider this when thinking about your own duty as an officer and as a warrior. Here is the golden opportunity to do what you have always known you were born to do. If you die, it is only the path to heaven- this should make you happy!

"But, if you choose not to fight, what is the benefit? What is the cost? I think you will be seen as a coward. I think you will be subjected to reprimand and punishment from your superiors, and insults from your fellow warriors. I think you will fall short of the knowledge you seek, and for that reason it will be a disservice to yourself as well as those who look to you for leadership. The enemy will think it was fear that drove you from the battlefield, rather than the compassion of an enlightened man. Since you rightly cherish that noble trait called honor, this will be a cross most impossible to bear.

"Look at the benefit of fighting in comparison. Die and you win heaven. Kill and you commit no sin because you destroy nothing under God. Win the battle and enjoy the Earthly rewards. It's all the same. There is nothing outside the Word of God, so resolve to fight!

"Now you are beginning to see the true nature of the immortal soul, but now let me tell you the true nature of action and reaction- of cause and effect. I know that you probably think you already know about it, but I will show you a new way to think about this idea. If you can understand it, you will be able to overcome your desires for the fruits of your actions.

"In this path, even an unsuccessful attempt is not in vain. It is the attempt itself which counts, so there cannot even be an adverse effect. Even a little effort will help you to overcome the terrible restraint of your own senses and Earthly perceptions.

"In this path, your will must become focused on one goal. If you do not have this focus and discipline, your mind will wander off in all directions after too many Earthly goals. Those who do not have the discipline may be able to quote scripture to the letter, but they do not know its inner truth. They are full of desire for rank in their church, or status in their community, and the rewards of heaven. They are good talkers, and can pull off all the elaborate rituals and memorized prayers which are supposed to bring them control over their surroundings, and an assured path to heaven, but they have missed the point. All they truly understand is the law of Cause and Effect, which chains men to an eternal death of their own creation.

"Those whose discipline is sapped away by exposure to such things really grow deeply attached to the pleasure and power that is promised here and in the hereafter. This constant desire for numerous things actually prevents them from developing the kind of concentration they need for directly experiencing God.

"The Western mind is full of subconscious and artificial divisions of reality, handed to us through myth and religion. Alchemy gives us the four elements which make up the world. Religion keeps us thinking about 'good and evil'. You, my friend, must overcome this tendency. You must overcome the idea that everything works in pairs of opposites- this polar thinking that prevents us from having a concept of a 'whole'. Keep your mind calm and tranquil. Even 'action and reaction' are pairs of opposites, and therefore artificial creations of our minds. It is an illusion that makes us think that we can understand the entire universe by studying all of the causes and effects- all of the pairs of opposites. You must remember the absolute certainty and indestructibility of the Word of God as an entirety, as one word, as 'Universe'.

"My point is this: To this desert we are sitting in, making a sandbox to play in is just superfluous. So, if you already have a simple and focused way to directly experience and know God, the Absolute Reality, all these comparisons of opposites are just a waste of time. To the enlightened person, even scripture is unnecessary.

"You have the right to the pursuit of happiness, as it says in the Declaration of Independence, but nowhere does it say you have a right to happiness. Desire for happiness can never be your motive. I think the Founding Fathers were pointing out that the virtue is in the pursuit and the labor, but not necessarily in the achievement of happiness. Of course, not only does this keep one from getting focused on greed and desire, but also keeps him from being lazy.

"Pursue your life with your heart focused on the One True God, and reject any claims of ownership on the happiness He provides you in the end. Keep equally stoic in the face of both failure and success, for they are both part of His plan, and your even-temper is the only way to walk the path He has set forth for you.

"If you worry about the results of your labor, your craftsmanship will be inferior compared to work done without such fears and anxiety. Take comfort that everything you do is contained within the ultimate plan of God. If you lose sight of this, and work only with the anxious expectation for results, you will be miserable.

"Even the popular polar idea of 'virtue versus vice' is artificially created in the minds of men, and therefore can be overcome in the peace of God. Therefore, devote yourself to achieving union with Him. What does this mean, if we are already a part of Him and his plan? It means that, rather than trying to do 'virtuous' deeds while avoiding 'vice', one should simply recognize how his heart and mind are united with God already- then simply act! In this simple peace of mind, it is easy then to reject the fruits of one's labors, which is one sure path to Light. The person who does this moves beyond the shackles of this mortal life and the limitations of the mind, and passes beyond even the concept of evil.

"When your intelligent mind can discard these deluded ideas of right and wrong actions, leading to good or bad results, you won't care at all about the outcome of any action, now or later. Now, you are confused because your mind is filled with conflicting scriptures, ideas, lessons, morals and myths that you have learned to give you answers and act as rules to follow in life. When your mind can focus without these distractions on the absolute reality that is God, then you will recognize the union that exists between you and Him."

Time seemed to stand still for A.J. that night in the desert as he listened to Chris's sermon. He was taken by a kind of magic that filled his soul with the tiniest glimmerings of Light, and he became hungry for more. He wanted to know everything about this "path" that Chris spoke of. He asked Chris if he had ever known anyone who had experienced this union with God, and how would he recognize such a person. How does he speak, or sit, or walk, and how will A.J. know if he experiences this union?

"It will be easy to know such a person," explained Chris, "because he knows the happiness of

God, and wants nothing else. Even though others may be tortured by desire, he simply disowns it. I would say that this person has squared himself with God and is truly awake. He is neither discouraged by adversity, nor longing for happiness. He is without fear, anger, and desire. I consider this person to be a seer, a true saint. He has escaped the chains of his mortal limitation and keeps a level head. If he is successful, he does not celebrate. If he fails, he does not mourn. This person is awakened.

"Just like a turtle can pull its legs into its shell, a saint can pull in his mortal senses. This person is awakened.

"The people who merely shun what they think is evil and wrong, and practice abstinence from these things, only run away from what they desire. Only when a person enters Reality does he actually leave desire in the past.

"Even the saints know that their mind and body are mortal and can therefore be led astray from the path. Even the seer knows that his senses are hard to control, but he tries, and calms his mind and focuses it on God. This person is awakened.

"If you think about all the stuff in your life, you will surely become attached to all that stuff. That attachment can become an addiction, and usually does. If you deny your addiction, just like a junkie, you will become enraged. As you well know, anger confuses the mind, which leads you to forget the lessons of your life-experience. When these lessons are gone, you have no more ability to discriminate between what is real and what is merely apparent. Without this ability, you will miss life's only purpose. I will talk about that more later.

"A.J., if you have no hatred and no desire, and you can walk around this world full of the objects of your hate and desire without any fear of either, you are only left with the peace and joy of God. Sadness then has no place, and your mind will be at peace.

"However, if your mind is undisciplined, you won't have the slightest notion that the reality of God is present everywhere and in all things. How could you even begin to contemplate this if your mind is constantly fixed on anger and lust, desire and hatred? Without the ability to contemplate calmly, there is no peace. Without peace, there is no happiness.

"Just like the wind can blow a sailboat off course, the mortal senses can blow the mind off course by exposing it to all the objects of his desire and hatred. One's better judgment blows off course right along with everything. When a person can still the winds of the senses, and calm the seas of the mind, I consider him to be awakened. His composed mind is awake in the knowledge of God. This knowledge of the Ultimate Reality, which flows through all things, is veiled in the darkness of night to the unknowing. The unknowing are awake only in the world of their mortal senses, which they mistake for the Light of day. To the seer, the awakened, that world is only darkness.

"Just like the river empties into the ocean, yet the ocean is largely undisturbed, so does desire flow into the saint, but he is not troubled. The wise man knows peace. The others are stirred up by their own lusts and hatred and cannot know peace. Both are cravings, the desire to control, just like ego and pride. They must be forgotten to be at peace.

"This, A.J., is what it means to be awakened in the knowledge of the Ultimate Reality. Once you can truly see this, you can never accidentally slip down into delusion again. Even in your time of dying, you will still experience the Light: You and God are One!"

The Path of Action

A.J. understood the concept Chris was talking about, and maybe even experienced a whiff of true understanding for a fraction of a second, but cynicism came barging in once again. "Isn't this hypocrisy?" asked A.J. aloud. "If this ultimate knowledge of God is a better way to live than any other way," he wondered, "then why are you encouraging me to fight and kill?"

"Remember," replied Chris reassuringly, "that I also explained the true nature of action and reaction, cause and effect. So it seems that the thoughtful person may choose the path of knowledge, while the active person may pick the path of action.

"Of course, we are all active to some extent every minute of every day. Even if you try to abstain from action, the attempt itself is an action. See? It is impossible not to act. Our minds are always working, our hearts always pumping- abstinence is a myth!

"Take, for example, a person who piously abstains from some physical 'sin' such as sex, but whose mind still dwells on the thought. This is actually quite normal, as many such people seek to renounce what they desire the most, maybe to prove that they have some measure of control over their lives. In any case, these folks are only fooling themselves. Their minds still act, and they are then forced into the act of abstinence by their own desire! It is the person who has glimpsed the true nature of Reality, the one focused on God, whose senses will become uninterested in such desires. It is this person who will not need to abstain because he will have no interest.

"I'm not saying that activity is a bad thing, of course. Activity is better than refusing to do anything. That's just lazy. You can't even feed yourself if you are lazy. I'm saying that it is a mistake to think that controlling your activity or the activity of others is a path to God. It is the opposite! It is through knowledge of the Ultimate Reality that you will have true self control, because there will be no shameful longing for you to suppress!

"I think this is where we need to talk about worship. Indeed, what IS worship? I think many people do not know the secret of worship, but let me tell you now: The world, and all of us in it, is bound by the shackles of our own activity. Worship can free us from this bondage. Worship is not throwing one's self at the feet of some invisible deity and providing it with adoration in hopes of a favor in return. Worship done like this, as a slave to a master, only strengthens the desire for results. No, it is rather the doing of an action as a sacrament- free from all hopes of results. It is the doing of an action only because it is a part of God's plan, and nothing more.

"In the beginning, God created man and set forth his duty on this Earth. With this duty was the promise of prosperity. Desire will ultimately be fulfilled by carrying out one's duties, rather than pursuing the desire itself. Fulfilling the requirements of duty honors the angels, and the angels will be gracious in turn. Thus, a man enters Heaven- the company of angels, and all his prayers will be answered. On the other hand, if a man prays, or gives tithes, or donates to charity, hoping that God will notice and grant him wishes, then he is truly a sinner. It is like a bachelor cooking for himself after work - usually the results are only intended to satisfy his hunger and the food is basic. This is because he is only cooking to feed his stomach. The reality is that praying, tithing, and charity work are all sacred unto themselves! They are *sacrament*! They are *ritual*! They ARE worship! There is nothing to expect beyond them. Just as the master chef prepares food out of love for preparing the food, and watching others enjoy what he has created, so must the seer prepare his ritual offerings for the sake of the preparation only. The prayers are made because God has set them forth in the Scriptures, so they are a sacred act deemed necessary by Him. This is only a symbol, alluding to the fact that all things under Heaven are God's work and are, therefore, necessary. If something is necessary, then the very act of doing the thing is worship. That which is sacred and eternal exists within each act as it is done, because it is part of the Cosmos, God's Will and Word. The blind only see 'doing' things, even good things, as a way to reach Heaven, but not as Heaven itself. This, A.J., is the secret of real worship.

"If a man refuses to act, or does things only in hopes of a sacred reward from God, he remains trapped in the endless cycle of his own desire and lust. He will never know what it is to not want - he will never see.

"There is even a deeper secret, A.J., beyond the true meaning of worship. I will unveil this to you now: Once you see that everything in the Cosmos follows the Divine Law, you will realize that nothing you do or do not do is outside the Will of God. Once you realize this, then you suddenly see that ritual, even rightly performed, is only a kind of practice. It trains the unseeing to see. It is an exercise. Ritual is intended to teach the practitioner and nothing more. It does not call down arcane powers, or speak to the angels, or bring one closer to the dead, but rather is a lesson with only one student in the classroom. Once you know the lesson, and know the true nature of worship, you no longer will need the instruction it offers. You will have nothing to gain from doing the ritual, or to lose by not doing the ritual. As the ritual represents all that is under Heaven, then nothing in the world can be gained or lost by your action or inaction under any circumstance. When you come to this understanding, you will be independent of everybody and everything. This is how a man reaches true freedom - true Heaven! You reach this truth by doing or not doing without worrying about the results. In fact, many saints have performed their work in exactly this spirit, as have many other enlightened souls. I once said to one such person about his work, "What reward shall I give thee

for all thy labor?" to which he selflessly responded,
"None but Thyself, O Lord!" Like him, your own work
should be done with no other desire than to inspire
others by your own sense of duty. This is the true
combat leader, and the true seer."

A.J. seemed not to notice that Chris had slipped
into the first person when describing his conversations
with past saints, but even if he had it would not have
seemed out of place that night. A.J. had been so
distressed earlier, and the entire conversation was so
engrossing, that it was almost as though he had slipped
into another world. To him, the cramped, hot turret of
the Abrams tank seemed as though it was the only place
in the Universe. It existed as a raft among the absolute
emptiness of deep space. In his mind, there was nothing
outside of his own thoughts and Chris's voice, gentle
and wise, flowing into the CVC helmet's speakers.

"Whatever you do as a great leader, your
soldiers will do as well," Chris continued. "I mean, look
at me. I have everything I need in life. There is nothing
I am lacking at all in the Universe. There is nothing
else out there somewhere that I need to make me happy,
but I keep working anyway. As a leader, if I work then
people will follow and do as I do, no matter what
direction I lead them. But, if I stop, everyone stops
because they are following my lead. If I stop, the world
comes to a stop.

"These people who do not see that duty is done
for its own sake, because to act is an inescapable

universal law, only perform their work in the hopes of reward. A man may work for money, food, love, and all of his needs. He attends his church in the hope of an everlasting reward after death. This seems like what is expected of him when he reads the holy texts and listens to his countrymen. But there is a deeper meaning to the words which he does not hear. This kind of duty, performed with an eye on a reward, is only duty done as a slave for a master. There will always be a hunger for the next meal, or the next forgiveness for his inevitable mistakes. So, he will always be a slave to these desires, never attaining the reward he seeks. The wise man, the seer, will do what is necessary only because it is necessary, and this will point others in the right direction – towards the true meaning of the sacred words! Simply leading by his example will teach the confused far more about this truth than trying to explain the words. He will show them how work is sacred by looking *beyond* the rewards brought by the work, fixing their attention on the Ultimate Reality of which their duty is a small part.

"The average person believes that he is the doer of things, like taking a bite of food, or making love, or enrolling in college, or turning right at the next street, or pulling the trigger on a gun. In his arrogance, he believes that these are his original ideas! How preposterous! A true seer knows that his life, his very thoughts and ideas, were set in motion with the beginning of the Universe. His lifespan, that part of the universe of which he is aware, is only a tiny scene in a vast play which stretches in all directions through the ages. He knows that his needs and desires are not a new invention in the vastness of time. He knows that his wants are not unique to him. The goals he seeks, and the decisions he makes to reach them, are shared by all and have been the same made by countless generations over the eons. He knows that his own lust for food, sex, recognition, etc., is inherited and that his mind will fix on the path to their satisfaction regardless of what he does about it. He knows that these needs existed before him as Universal laws, just as the objects of these desires exist as part of the Universe. Therefore, the wise know that needs are merely the Universe attaching itself to the Universe. With this wisdom, he can observe this transaction with detachment and not get tied up in his own desires.

"This doesn't mean that you should just throw your hands up in the air in futility, saying that nothing you do or do not do matters. The unseeing, who do not share your deeper understanding of the nature of duty, will simply follow you into laziness without being freed from their desires. They think God is the fulfillment of their desire, when you know that God is both the fulfillment AND the desire itself! Keep your mind focused on this: That nothing, NOTHING you do or avoid doing is outside of the God of Nature. With that single insight, you can move forward freely to do your duty. If you let yourself, for one second, doubt what I have said here, and do not understand that your mind's attraction to certain things and aversion to other things

is perfectly natural, then you risk failing in your duty.
A.J., you are a warrior. That is your duty. The pacifist is
another person with another duty. If you must die,
prefer to die doing your duty and not someone else's."

A.J. thought about this for a long moment,
absently picking at the rubber eyepiece of the .50 caliber
"Ma Deuce" machinegun's periscope sight which hung
before him in the turret. The fatalism of the whole thing
bothered him immensely. He could grasp that a soldier
must embrace the situation in which he has found
himself, and find it within himself to do his duty. That
seemed like a reasonable choice which could naturally
follow from what Chris had just said. But, he thought,
how was this kind of killing different than criminal
murder? How, in the grand scheme of things, is it any
morally different? He thought for another moment,
then posed the question to Chris, "If the end result of all
of your spiritual thought and deep understanding is the
killing of fellow human beings, how is that any different
than the evil deeds of murderers? If my killing is done
by 'choice', then how is it that men seem compelled to
kill by impulse, as if they are driven to evil against their
will?"

Chris replied, "You have stumbled on the very
nature of good and evil. Indeed, why is your killing
'good' and that of the murderer 'evil'? Yours, A.J., is
based on choice – the choices you made have created this
inescapable situation for you, and require you to carry
out the duty you chose in the first place. Nothing more.
You can also choose to not kill, or to stop the killing

and take prisoners when the situation warrants. You can choose to show restraint, mercy, kindness - all of these even in the awful face of battle. Your murderous enemy cannot. Your real enemies are rage and lust. These two emotions blind the thoughts of those who would murder. When these take over, there is no more clear thought from the higher brain, but only the most basic instincts of the lower parts of our being. When rage and lust take over, the other functions of the mind become its slave, feeding the fire even more. One so afflicted can no longer discriminate between what is real and what is merely apparent. The murderer has lost all judgment and restraint. He cannot cease his actions because they were not of his choosing. He will not show restraint on the battlefield, or mercy, or kindness. He will destroy indiscriminately, target civilians wantonly, murder prisoners of war, desecrate holy places - this is the evil caused by rage and lust. You are not like this, A.J. Your violence is focused on the enemy, avoiding undue damage to civilians and shrines, yielding to your will. This is why your killing is 'good'. This is why you must fight. This is why you must win!

"It is this will of yours that controls your mind and senses, which allows you to see the Divine Reality I have already taught you. Your will is above all of this material world, your senses which connect your mind to that world, and ultimately your mind which ponders the world. It is your will that is closest to the Divine Reality! It is the observer in you which observes the thinking mind! Use it to control the mind and destroy your enemies: rage and lust."

Salvation through Knowledge

Then Chris said something truly troubling to A.J. "This same knowledge of the Divine Reality is something I once taught to Saint Paul. It was to be handed down through the ages, from teacher to student, but it became forgotten along the way."

A.J.'s head throbbed and swam as he tried to comprehend what he had heard. He knew that it could not be, but his heart told him that there could be no doubt. The manner in which Chris had been talking all night, the tempo and gravity of his voice, and the strange sensation of isolation felt there in the desert night had all conspired to bathe him in a new reality- one not of this world. A.J. knew that he was in another time, a different consciousness, and Chris was somehow the cause of this condition. But, he *had* to ask the question that came to his mind, though he both knew and feared the answer. He had known the answer, perhaps for quite some time, and feared it all the same because the answer would be beyond comprehension and sanity.

"Chris," his voice emanated weakly above his sprinting heart, "how can I believe this, since Saint Peter lived two thousand years ago- before you were born?"

"You and I," Chris replied, as a kind teacher to a small child, "have both existed for a very long time.

That is, the stuff that makes us- atoms, energy, the very breath within our lungs- has come to us by a process which started with the beginning of time. You and I, A.J., exist as if riding the crest of a wave of time stretching back to the beginning. The only difference between you and me is that I can see this and you cannot." He paused, the words bouncing around A.J.'s head, trying to find a home among other, more rational thoughts.

"With this knowledge," Chris continued, "I know that I cannot point to a time when I was ever born, or will ever die. This way of looking at my life, as the entire wave stretching in all directions through time, makes me the Lord of everything that lives. Sure, it looks like there are countless births and deaths along the way, but I know that I am an unbroken being throughout all of this. With this knowledge, I am the master of my own creation- I am the creation itself! I was formed long ages ago, at the very beginning, when the world came to be. The crest we ride is the ripple of the consciousness, the present, a fleeting moment.

"When there is evil at hand, and the righteous need strength and wisdom, I return. I come in every age to save the holy, destroy sin, and to shine a Light. He who knows this, my true nature, knows that he too shall never die, but have everlasting life. This same nature of his own being returns to me. When he departs from fear, lust and anger, he will take sanctuary in me. In this knowledge, he will be safe, purified, and at home.

Whatever he wishes is also my wish. Whatever he receives is my gift. Wherever he walks, I am with him.

"Now, A.J., here is the point to all of this talk: Men worship and pray, more often than not, to alter their material world in their favor- call it a material gain. This is an easy enough accomplishment in the material world, regardless! Now, you understand that my true nature is beyond all of this material. You know that I am the author of the material, the actions, the changes- though I, myself, am changeless. Since this is the case, my present body and consciousness merely being a ripple in the vast ocean of my true self, I have no desire for the fruits of my actions. There is no need for such things! If you understand this, A.J., you will never be a slave to your own actions. The ancients knew this, and you must as well.

"You must know the true nature of action, itself. This knowledge is true liberation, and it can be difficult to understand. The litmus test for the presence of this knowledge in your mind is when you are able to see that there is a kind of action in inaction, and a kind of inaction in every action. When you can see this, you will be able to do either with a detached tranquility that is the liberation from action. You will be able to act without the thirst for the result, without scheming, and without sin. The knowledge of my true nature and the nature of action breaks the chain which binds you to your lust for the material. It is enough. You will abandon wish-thinking, which serves only to weigh down your life. You will truly possess nothing. God will give and take away, pain and pleasure will cycle through your life, you will win some and lose some- and you will not be troubled. This chain being broken frees your heart to really live, filling with Light. All of your actions will be the ritual of the True Worship I spoke of. If this becomes the case, nothing you do can be evil! I say again, God is the ritual, the offering, the fire, and the person making the offering- He is everywhere in every action!

"There are many people with many different rituals and ways of worship. With your new knowledge you may now have a deeper understanding of these actions so that you might, by contrast, always recognize the True Worship I have just described.

"Some people merely worship the angels, saints, prophets, faeries, and gods set before them. Others at least contemplate the relationship of the soul with the god. Either way, these people are making the soul the offering and their god becomes the fire to which it is offered. Can you understand this?

"The ascetics, in their quest for enlightenment, harshly treat their senses and practice restraint in all of their contacts with the world outside of their minds. These people make their own senses the offering, and the self-discipline is the sacrificial fire.

"In contrast, there are those who see God in everything, drinking in all manner of pleasures with their senses. These hedonists make the things they see, smell, taste, and feel into objects of sacrifice, while their enjoyment is the fire into which it is all thrown and devoured.

"There are yet others, of whom I am sure you are aware, who renounce all actions in the world, and sit in quiet contemplation. For them, their actions are the sacrifice and their sacrificial fire is the nearness to God they obtain.

"There are many other ways to worship, of course. Some renounce action AND possessions, among other deprivations they may impose upon themselves. Some practice Yoga, and others study scriptures or join strict monastic orders. Breathing exercises, fasting to weaken desire- a thousand ways to worship! Of course, all of these people understand sacrificial worship. They are all absolving sins, gaining immortality, having prayers answered. Their worship makes them happy on Earth. This is important, because if you can't even find happiness in this life what can you expect from any other?

"As you can see, all of these methods of worship involve some sort of action. It is when you may worship *without* action that you are truly free. When you can simply contemplate God, without ritual and its apparent benefits, then your every action becomes True Ritual. Your reward, without desiring it, will be enlightenment. There are others who are thus enlightened, and you should seek them out and learn from them. When you become enlightened, you will never return to darkness. With this knowledge, you will see plainly that your true nature is the same as mine which I have described to you. I am all of creation, and so are you. There is no separation between you and God, between the material world and the divine.

"With this knowledge, there is no sin you can commit, A.J., here in this war or in any other place or time. Though you may have to kill, or do other deeds, you do so without lust and greed- your motives are pure and therefore aligned with Truth and God's Will. Actions made in this state cannot be sinful. It is simply not possible. If you embrace this knowledge, and hold it in your heart, you can immediately- this instant- rise to the highest and purest heights to which a man or woman may rise. Those who are ignorant of this knowledge are doomed to live a life chasing after desires: unanswered prayers, unfulfilled wishes, unanswered questions. They will not see that the filling of one of these voids leads only to the awareness of the next need or want. This hell never ends for them.

"Ah, but I can still see doubt deep within your heart, A.J. You doubt it can be that easy. You doubt the obvious truth of what I say, though it is right before you. This doubt emanates from your inner desire- a desire for things to remain confused! You *know* your confused state. It is a warm bath, a comfortable chair. It is home to you. You don't want to leave it! But, A.J., this is only self-delusion. It is only a comfortably furnished prison cell!

"There is something else deep in your heart. This I know. You are of a rare kind, with a special gift. You were born with the powerful sword called *gnosis*! This is the power to distinguish between what is real and what is only apparent. Where is your sword now? Draw it and kill delusion! Then stand up and take action!"

The Path of Liberation

A.J. recognized this gnosis within himself. Even as a child, he had a rare gift to see through lies and to sense when other people were deceiving themselves. He had what could be called a very acute sense of Truth. But, as he listened to Chris, he became confused about the seeming contradiction set before him. After pausing to organize his dilemma into words he began, "Chris, you tell me on one hand that I must seek liberation from action, yet on the other hand you keep encouraging me to fight. Tell me which is better. What path should I follow?"

Chris spoke again, "My friend, the point is not whether or not you act or do not act. That is immaterial. What matters is the *intent* behind the act. When this intent is correct, both acting and not-acting bring the liberation I spoke of. Either of these, with the right motive, is better than merely refusing to do something. After all, refusing to do something IS doing something! You are simply replacing one action with another, thinking you are doing nothing. It is a kind of trap your mind can fall into. Actually, to ignore something passionately, or to shun it, is really giving it one hundred percent of your attention- taking all of your mental effort! And there you are, stuck in the same trap of action.

"When you can do or not do something, either way, without hatred and desire being the motive, it leads to liberation. When you stop running away from the thing you hate, and stop running towards the thing you desire, your man-made manacles of delusion are broken. Only the unwise think that action and inaction are two different things. Or, in other words, they think that action and the true knowledge of God I just spoke of are opposites. You will find, to the contrary, that both of these paths lead to the same place- are the same path! For example, let's say you wanted to seek Truth and God through meditation only, without action. Well, it will take a lot of discipline -that is, ACTION- to get yourself to a state of meditation. When you see that action and inaction are united under God's plan, and so too are you a part of that plan, as are all things you can find in the Universe, then you are able to act knowing your motive is also one with the plan- untainted by lust and rage.

"This is the true meaning of the phrase "to act without sin". When you act without sin, your heart beats with God's, and your actions are naturally part of his Will. When you can see that no matter what you do- eat, sleep, blink, run, sit, listen to music, et cetera- is all going to happen whether you will it or not, you will see that it is only natural that you do these things. When you see this, you will realize that you are not separate from the Universe, but PART OF IT! Like the Earth goes around the sun, so too does your body run its course according to Nature- listening to music, sleeping, and all that. Your mind, too, works according to the Law of Nature in the exact same way. When you put away things that drive your desire, like anger and longing, then your mind clicks clearly into place with the rest of the Universe. All actions become the God-offering we spoke of earlier, and you can do actions without them trapping you and running your life for you. Otherwise, when your desires start to decide what actions you will take, then you become stuck in the mental trap once again- a slave.

"Now, A.J., let me tell you of the true happiness that can be found here. When you can know that your body and its senses are going to go right on ahead doing what your body does and sensing what it will, and you have used your gnosis to see that your mind and thoughts are truly no different, all of your actions and inactions will flow naturally. You will not be trapping yourself, and you won't be dragging others into your trap with you. You might say that your anger and desire are also part of God's plan, and that the trap was set by Him. But, the Universe works *exactly as it should* and your mind is a part of it! It would be the height of self-centered whining to say that you were created with intentional flaws, with sin. Take responsibility for how you view the world! It is in your own head only that you imagine you *will* things to be done. Would a perfect God, everywhere and all-powerful, care to trap you in a petty mind game? Would he care if you sinned in that way? Indeed, would he care about this kind of righteousness in all of mankind?

"Think of it this way, the true nature of the Universe, Truth, is like a brilliant Light. Between our minds and that Light is a veil of darkness that is of our own making. It is born from our own limitations. We fill this dark area with our delusion, myths, superstitions and dreams.

"When we seek the Light, we must destroy the delusion between. Once we move from darkness to Light, it shines from us like the sun- the true nature of God revealed! One who sees this Light can surely never turn away from it. They dwell with God, knowing him always in their heart. When this Truth is known, it becomes the only aim, and action falls by the wayside. Here is true liberation and redemption from past malice, in word and deed. Here the seeker shall stay forever.

"Is this not truly heaven? With this Truth all Earthy things are of equal value, from the greatest to the lowliest. Surrounded by the Light of God, the world is conquered! Even walking the globe as a live human being, the enlightened knows the Truth is everywhere, unchanging, without evil- here in the real world! This person does not flail about in rapturous displays of faith and ecstasy, but rather carries with him a certain stoicism. He is calm, clear minded, neither too excited about good things nor depressed about bad things. His consciousness can look towards the Light of Truth and away from every-day objects, taking happiness from this knowledge. If he were to give too much value to the objects of his desire they would soon become objects of sorrow, because the pleasure he gets from them would soon diminish. This never-ending start and stop of pleasure brings no real pleasure to those who know Truth.

"And, this heaven I speak of, this happiness, it is to be had here on Earth before death! Right here and now, it is possible to master the cravings and the lust and the hatred and all of that which deludes us. We can see the Light, the Truth, God- now! This can only be done by looking at your own delusions, the darkness between you and the Light, and destroying them. Those who dash delusion to bits and see the Light have their flaws destroyed in that moment. Confident, their senses mastered, they become bound to the welfare of their fellow creatures.

"Even those who suppress the deluded self through meditation to find this Truth beyond, who slow the mind, who check their thoughts, who seek to be free of their psyches, putting aside fear, putting aside anger, putting aside desire, become free.

"No matter what path is taken to the Light of Truth, it will lead to the author of everything, of every bounty and of every famine, God of the worlds, and friend to all men. I say to you A.J, who would not want this peace?"

The Path of Contemplation

A.J. used the commander's override controls to slew the turret and gunsight, surveying the enemy just ahead of him in the darkness. Chris continued to talk gently into the tank's com system, "If you can do your duty without an eye on promotions, medals, pay, or even victory, you are a true stoic- a true monk. But, if you merely follow your orders to the letter, simply by rote or habit, selfish, dodging your real duty, then you are no monk at all. You have to understand that even what is fashionably called 'meditation' these days is really just avoidance of duty. People who practice this cannot know the path of action because they are preoccupied with the results of their actions- anxious about their future. They can, however, reach very near Truth and Light in this way, but when the time to grasp it is near they will eventually have to dispense with their own acts, and become tranquil. Not only is this the final step in reaching that liberated state, but it is the very definition of that state!"

Chris went on, "This brings up the question: How should one use one's own will? What is 'will' in the first place? First, let me say that willpower should be used to uncover the Truth, not to hide it under desire and actions- want and ritual. The human will is the only friend to God, and also his only enemy. This is because when a person is self-controlled, that person is a friend to Truth. But, the will is turned hostile toward the

Truth in people who possess no self-control. It is only
the serene one, absorbed in Truth, who masters the will.
This person is unflinching in heat or in cold, in pain or
in pleasure, in honor or dishonor.

"All it takes is one time for a person to reach
fulfillment through the knowledge and personal
experience of God's True Nature and that person can
never again be moved by the mere desires of the senses.
Mud, stone, and gold have the exact same value to one
who masters the senses in such a way. Such an
individual has, indeed, realized his or her union with the
Universe- a union that was present all along! This
realization allows one to regard equally friends and
comrades, foe and kinsmen, the vile, the wicked, those
who would judge others, and those who belong to none
of these categories.

"However, if you want to practice meditation, I
will tell you the true way. To prepare, you should find a
solitary place, alone. Give thought to what I have told
you about exercising control over your mind and your
body. Free yourself from hopes and worldly possessions
for a while. Meditate on Truth unceasingly. To begin,
sit somewhere firm, in a seat neither too high nor too
low, and located somewhere clean and uncluttered. You
may even cover your seat with a soft cloth to make it
comfortable. Now, sit there and begin to hold the senses
and imagination in check- keep the mind concentrated
upon Truth. This kind of concentration is exceedingly
difficult at first, but it will work- your heart will become
pure. Your posture will be motionless, with your body,

head, and neck erect. Your vision will be a little drawn inward, as if you are gazing at the tip of your nose in a relaxed manner. Do not look around your surroundings while doing this. Once you reach a serene and fearless state, firm in your will to hold your senses and Earthly desires in check, focus on Me as the only desire, the only struggle, dissolving and merging into Truth- your only prize and purpose.

"The Seeker who achieves perfect control over the mind in this way, and struggles continuously, will discover the perfect unity with the Universe- the crowning peace of Heaven- the Peace that is Me. This practice of meditation is not for the person who overeats or who intentionally under-eats. It is not for the person who sleeps too much or who stays up all night. Moderation, rather, is the key in all things such as eating, sleeping, and recreation. For this person, meditation is the path to contentment.

"A.J., this may lead you to ask 'When can a person be said to have achieved perfect union with God?' The answer is when the mind is under perfect control and freed from all desires so that he or she becomes absorbed in the Universe. Nothing else will do! As Wadsworth said, "…undisturbed; As on the pavement of a Gothic church walks a lone monk, when the service hath expired, in peace and silence." He described perfectly the single-mindedness of the True Seeker who meditates upon Truth. It is only when, through the practice of meditation, the mind becomes still that the monk can know God. The person is then satisfied entirely by this happiness that can only be realized by the heart, yet is entirely beyond the grasp of the normal senses. The monk stands firm in this realization of the innermost Truth, unwavering from this discovery forever and ever. This self-knowledge is the most valuable kind of treasure, beyond anything else. It is a new kind of faith that is so certain that it can never be broken, even by the deepest sorrow, and requiring no effort to keep once gained.

"In fact, to achieve this certainty is to finally understand the real meaning of the word *faith*. Faith means to break contact with pain. You must practice it with purpose and without losing confidence. Renounce all of your Earthly desires forever because they come from an undisciplined will. Use your gnosis to rein in your whole wild pack of senses. With patience and the application of your intelligent will, you will free yourself from all mental distractions. You must fix your mind upon the Ultimate Reality, never fixating on anything else, even if your mind strays or becomes involved in your daily tasks. You must always draw it back and make it submit to Truth only.

"Your mind will become utterly quiet and devoid of passions, knowing the Ultimate Reality- the highest bliss. Your mind will also become free of evil while in constant contemplation. The way is easy for those touched by God in this way. The happiness is eternal. Your heart will be in Light, causing your eyes to see the Universe in all things equally and without boundary. You will see in every living thing that part of the

Universe that is eternal within yourself. Indeed, you will see all Creation within your own eternal self, as well.

"The Devout Seekers see Me in all things, and all things within Me. They never lose sight of Me and I never lose sight of them. They are firm in their union with Me, worshiping my presence in all beings. Such a Seeker lives within Me, no matter where he or she is in life. It is these people, who share the happiness and sorrow of every creature in their own hearts as if it were their own, who I proclaim to have achieved the highest faith."

A.J. thought about this for a long, silent moment in his half-dream world. What Chris had just said to him about this 'meditation' seemed impossible for anyone to achieve. It struck him as unrealistic that a person with any sense of responsibility to his fellow creatures should just throw all his stuff in the garbage and say '*Om*' on a mountain top for the rest of his life. A.J. posed the question to Chris, "You say that meditation is a state of constant knowledge of my unity with everything else, but I don't see how anyone can do that all the time. I mean, there are so many day-to-day responsibilities and distractions, and anyway the mind wanders whether you want it to or not. Take this war, for example: How am I to remain 'focused on God' when a mortar round lands next to me or someone is shooting at me? My senses tend to take over, to say the least. And, what about sex drive, hunger, and all those quite normal and healthy desires that keep us alive and keep the species going? Nobody has been able to tame that! I think you'd have more luck spitting in the wind."

"Yes," Chris responded without hesitation, "the mind is very restless and, without a doubt, hard to discipline. However, it can be controlled through constant practice and calculated dispassion. Of course, if a person has no self-control this kind of practice will be very, very difficult. But anyone with a sliver of self-discipline can master it through diligence and proper practice. After all, it is only one of several paths a person can take."

A.J. quickly followed up, "Yah, but let's say someone has faith, you know, but just doesn't have it in them to struggle hard enough. Say this person has a naturally wandering mind and keeps failing at meditation. What then? Does that person go to hell or something? What I'm saying is, I've always been taught that when a person goes astray from the path of God he screws up both lives- the physical and the spiritual. That person has no salvation and is as lost as anything. This is what bothers me about what you were saying, Chris."

Even though it didn't before seem possible to A.J., Chris's voice became even more soothing and placid, seeming almost to emanate from within his own head, "No, my son. That person is not lost, either in this world or the next one. No Seeker of Truth ever comes to an evil end, for it is true that they shall not perish, but have life everlasting. A person who practices meditation, or any path to Truth for that matter, and falls away from their practice will achieve the same Heaven as the doers of good deeds- reborn in this life or the next. This can only lead to a redoubling of the person's gnosis and will to truly know the Ultimate Reality. Because of their earlier attempts, such people will be even closer to Truth in this new existence, because they cannot 'un-know' what they have already learned. They will be driven despite themselves! I say that any person who has even once asked the way to God goes farther than anyone who merely recites prayers and performs rituals. This is a process of constant reinvention of the self, removing impurities to reach the highest state at last.

"Great are those who simply seek to be with God. They are greater than those who subdue the body through pain. They are greater than those who are only religious scholars. They are even greater than the merely charitable, though charity lasts beyond the grave. Therefore, A.J., become a Seeker no matter your fears of failure. For, whoever dedicates their hearts to me, worshiping me in faith and in love, is among the highest who I call my very own."

Knowledge and Experience

"Devote your whole mind to Me," Chris went on, "and practice your gnosis. See Me as your only refuge. By doing these things you can, without a doubt, come to know Me in My true form. I will tell you how. I will give you both the conventional form of knowledge and the direct spiritual experience. When you have that, there is nothing else in the World that is unknown to you. How many even seek this chance, let alone receive the opportunity? Maybe one person out of thousands? And, from among those Seekers of Truth, how many will ever see my absolute true form? Maybe just one.

"The alchemists of old have said that My true composition is of the five elements: earth, air, fire, water, and ether. Additionally, they ascribed to Me the three elements of the mind, the intellect, and the ego. You must understand that behind these eight symbols, and distinct from them, is That which is the basic consciousness of all beings, and the source of all life- sustaining the entire Universe! You must know this Underlying Truth that is Me, one and the same. It is the womb of all things. I am the birth and death of the Cosmos. I am the *primum mobile*- the only source and cause. There are no others before Me. All of the worlds in all of the galaxies in the Cosmos are held upon my shoulders. I am the spirit of the water, the sun and moon, the Amen in the prayer, the Holy Word of God. It is My nature that vibrates throughout the dimensions of reality, alive in all people. I am the smell of the soil, the light of fire, the suffering of the saints- all lives live within Me. Recognize me as the eternal seed of all that grows, and the intelligence of those who understand. I am the vigor of the active and the strength of the strong. I am all that people can imagine and desire within the Laws of Nature- devoid of lust and craving.

"It is important that you know even the states of confusion and darkness flow from Me, but you will not find Me in them. The whole world is deluded by these, which are merely moods and states-of-mind. It is only this darkness that prevents everyone in the world from seeing Me in my true form. I am beyond the darkness, supreme and eternal. I know that it is hard to see this, A.J., being born into a natural state of confusion. However, if you take solace within Me only, you will pass beyond the darkness into Light. Those who do evil in this world will remain deluded, turning away from Me, lowly among all people. They have lost their clear judgment in the maze of confusion. They behave not like humans, but like animals or demons instead.

"There is more to know about people, my A.J. You must recognize that I have four types of worshipers. Some are simply world-weary, and seek a bliss beyond this physical life. Some seek knowledge, a laudable pursuit of course. Others, still, seek happiness- also a worthwhile goal. However, it is the fourth kind of person, those who possess the spiritual gnosis I told you about earlier, who are the highest of these. It is these people, who can distinguish the real from the merely

apparent, who are continuously united with Me. By
their nature, they are devoted to Me, alone, and no
other. They are dear to me. Of course, the other three
types of Seekers are very good as well, but it is in the
Gnostics that I see My Self. The other three may love
me for what I can offer them, but it is the Gnostic who
loves me for my very nature alone. It is through
repeated reinvention of the self, a cycle of death and
rebirth, that these people strengthen their gnosis. They
make Me their final goal, and then surpass *that* desire -
to take refuge in Me. They know that I am all there is-
rare and great are these men and women!

"It is only those who have a gnosis blinded by
the darkness of earthly desire that establish all the
various rituals and cults. They worship various deities
for whatever reason is in their nature. You must
understand, however, that it does not matter what god a
person chooses to worship. If one has even a little faith,
I make that faith strong. With this, the worshiper's
prayers are answered. What they do not know is that I
stand behind the idol as the only source. Often, people
of little understanding pray for fleeting, worldly items
and interventions. If this is their only goal to worship,
that's the only reward they will get. It is only those who
seek Me who will come to Me.

"It is ignorant to think that I, the Ineffable and
Formless, have ever become human. Those who think
this obviously do not know my true nature, one with all
Reality, changeless and beyond merely human. This
human form is only My illusion. How could anyone of

this world, confused and bewildered as they are by their own delusions, ever recognize me- birthless, deathless, changeless? I, A.J., know all beings past, present, and future! No one can know me. This ignorance is natural, though, as creatures are misled from the moment they are born by the illusion that the world they see is all of reality in its entirety. The delusion comes from their own hatred, lust, and desire. But those who do good to others in this world are freed from this delusion. It is the Gnostic who sees clearly that all they can possibly know of this world is merely a faint fingerprint of the Ultimate Reality! These people remain steadfast in their will and worship Me.

"People often take comfort in Me to ease their fear of aging and of death. Even in this way, they may know Truth, the true nature of their eternal selves, and the creative power that is within God. Knowing Me in this way they can eventually grasp the difference between the real and the apparent natures of Reality, the place of the individual within the Universe, and the true nature of God. Even on their deathbeds whereon they must expire, as it was once said, they continue to know Me. In that time, they are brought into Me."

The Way to Eternal God

A.J. thought about all that Chris said for what seemed to him a very long time. He had no way of knowing that time had no meaning in this moment, in the presence of Truth. All he could do was to ask the questions that had, as he was surprised to discover, churned and battled within him for so long. "Tell me," he said, "what is God? What is the soul? What is the creative power of God? Explain to me further this illusion of a world, and our place in it. Who is this God who seems to rule over all the actions of the body? If he is in me, how is it possible? At the moment of death, how do you show yourself to people who are about to be united with you?"

"God," Chris began, "is that which is unchanging and independent of any cause outside of itself. When we think of God as dwelling within an individual, we call it the soul. The creative power of God is the Word, causing all things to come into being. The nature of this illusory world is constant change. The place of mankind within the Universe is consciousness of the self and, therefore, of the Universe. I alone, who sits here now in this tank, am God who reigns over all action. At the hour of death, a person who has sought Me throughout life will, without doubt, dwell upon Me and be united with Me. It is, therefore, important that you do your duty. If you set yourself to knowing Me in life, you will come to Me in death. Of this there is no doubt. Practice your meditation, whatever it may be, and do not be distracted. You will, in the end, come to the Lord Most High, source of all Light. Words cannot describe the all-knowing God, lord of all kings, ageless, ungraspable by the cleverest of minds- the Grand Architect of the Universe, shining and self-luminous like the sun rising in the east. Who could know this true form of God? God is beyond the darkness and delusion of mankind.

"Now, let me tell you a little about the Eternal God. Those who can break the shackles of desire are united with God at that moment. These people practice control of their passions. When this self-control is practiced for many years without distraction of the mind, I am easily attained at death. Indeed, I was never apart from them in life. The reuniting of a soul with Me is the ultimate perfection. Once united with Me, there is no longer a need for the constant reinvention of the self, no need for the transience of life and all its pain. Without this ultimate unity, even the realms of Heaven would be subject to the constant cycle of rebirth, reinvention, death, and birth again.

"The Universe can be thought of as having a day and a night. In the dawn of day, all life begins and comes into the flesh- mortal. As night falls, all life must dissolve back into atoms. This, A.J., is life as you see it- appearing, disappearing, unceasing with the cycles of day and night. All are helpless within this cosmic procession of ages, so they do the best that they can. But behind this cycle of lives coming into existence and disappearing back out of existence lies another Reality-eternal and changeless. It is not subject to this cosmic cycle of day and night. Some call it Ineffable. To reach this Reality is the greatest achievement of all mankind. It is My highest state of being. Here is perfect union with God. It can only be attained through devotion to the Truth within which all living things exist and by which the Universe is filled.

"So, here I have shown you two clear paths. You can choose either. The path of darkness leads back to yet another death and subsequent rebirth of the self, hoping your gnosis has strengthened in the process. The other is the path of Light, as if it were the six months of the summer sun rising in the east, standing at high meridian in the south, and setting in the west. It is like the moon waxing to bright fullness. The Seeker who takes this path goes to God. These two paths have existed since time immemorial, time without beginning. Once you know them, you can never be misled. Though scriptures of many kinds may say that Heaven can be reached by studying holy books, performing rituals, practicing self-denial, and giving to charity, it is the Seeker who understands what I have just said who will gain more than any who only follow those scriptural teachings. That person will reach the source of all things, the highest house of God."

Matter and Spirit

"There is something I wish to know," A.J. began again, hardly believing the opportunity for knowledge that lay before him, "I hear a lot of talk of 'spirit' or 'spiritual', or even 'soul', but how is that different than the matter of the body? How can a body know itself? What even is knowledge, and what is it that needs to be known?"

"The body," Chris began, "is a thing that can be known, like a farmer knows the field. He can, for example, plant crops in the field and watch them grow – harvesting after a long season. It is the wise ones who know that the Soul of a person is much like this farmer, but watching dispassionately and experiencing what takes place in the body instead of in a field. Now, simply recognize that I am the Soul in everybody. To know the difference between the Knower and that which is Known is the highest knowledge."

Chris paused, not to think, but only to allow his words to sink in, then continued, "I will tell you exactly what the Known is: It is Nature, Change, and Genesis. I will also tell you about the Soul, and how as the Knower of what is Known it has many powers. The saints and holy ones throughout the ages have described these eternal truths in many ways, in song, in scripture, in poetry – sublime in their ability to convey the wisdom. They describe the world of matter, or the 'profane' as some would have it, as the Cosmos in both its physical matter and hidden forces. In these songs it is the intellect, the ego, the five elements, the bodies of men and animals, the knowing and the doing of men and animals, the mind itself, the unceasing input from the senses, love, hate, wanting, pain, pleasure, and even the very consciousness and will of man – all churning, changing, and bounded within the human being. Therefore, be humble! Do no harm. Don't be pretentious. Be honorable and have forbearance towards others. Serve your teachers with devotion. Keep both your mind and your body clean of impurity. Be calm and resolute. Set aside your ego and stand aside from yourself and all that your senses desire – the true meaning of ecstasy. Know the frailty of life, and how it is chained to the cycle of birth, age, suffering, and death. Be a slave to nothing! Covet no one or no thing to please you or to fill your home. Approach both pain and pleasure with detachment. Love only Me, free of all these distractions! Enjoy solitude more than the commotion of crowds. Tirelessly seek to know the Soul, and to know why you seek it in the first place. This, A.J., is true wisdom. The only thing keeping people from such wisdom is ignorance.

"Now, apart from all this," Chris made a small gesture towards the stretch of open desert to his side, "is the knowledge of the transcendent, the eternal, without beginning or end – beyond not only all that is, but beyond all that is not. Knowledge of this leads to everlasting life. He exists and experiences all things everywhere, yet He Himself is not bounded by mere senses, or the objects of desire and confusion that they bring. He senses them, but is free from them. He is all-pervasive, within and without everyone and everything – living or inert. His presence is the most subtle, so far distant that people grope for Him in vain, yet He is not far from each one of us. He is a single and perfect whole, yet appears to us as a Universe of unending shapes and creatures. He is the Creator, Sustainer, and Destroyer of all of this that appears to us! He is the Light, beyond our comprehension in ignorant darkness. He is Knowledge, the one real thing we may study and be certain of in our hearts. Now you have learned what Knowledge is, and also what needs to be Known, and the true nature of the Knower. Those who have this wisdom are ready to attain union with Him, that they may be made perfect in One.

"Understand, though, that both Cosmos and God are without beginning. All of evolution and all objects of the senses flow forth from Cosmos, to include the evolution of the body and of the senses, themselves. It is this sense of the self as a separate, evolved object among the whirlwind of other creatures and objects in the Cosmos that is the source of our pleasure and of our pain. You see, we mistake our individual selves who experience this world as just another Cosmic object, but really the True Knower is the Soul – and God is the Soul within everybody, the actual Knower. If we exist in the state of mistaken identity, our individual selves will continue to seek a feeling of wholeness by uniting with other like-objects in a state of constant, unquenchable desire. However, the reality is that God exists in us as if a silent witness to our lives, making all actions possible, sanctioning our decisions, and experiencing our experiences. This Soul is limitless and supreme. One who has directly experienced God within himself or herself and knows Him to be beyond mere matter and confusion will have everlasting life. Some can achieve this experience through contemplation, others through meditation. Some others will experience Him through simply living a good and pure life, acting rightly. Even those who do not or cannot experience God in these ways, but rather practice prayers and rituals by rote as they have been taught, will also never die.

"A.J., I will reveal to you this: All of Creation that you can experience flows forth from the apparent union between the Knower and That which is Known — between Cosmos and the Divine. One who truly understands this will see the Lord in every creature, eternal and deathless even in mankind. Aware of His omnipresent nature, the true seer will never offend his or her own Soul that is the face of God. Once ego falls away and reveals this true face, the highest bliss is possible. This true seer will know that all action is taken by the material body, and that the Soul is without action. A person who sees the lives of all creatures as contained within and created by Him will also find Him. The Soul is eternal, changeless, beyond crass desire — impartial to the fruits of our actions and unblemished even though it is housed within our bodies. As the sun

rises in the east, so too does the Knower, illuminating
all that is Known. To use this wisdom of the Knower
and That which is Known is to find freedom from the
toils of the material world and achieve the highest goal."

The Three Delusions

"I will show you even more wisdom," Chris went
on, "that is of the highest order. It is the kind that, when
discovered by the saints, set them free of their mortal
bodies. Once free, they lived as One with Nature, with
life everlasting through the turning ages – even free
from the destruction at the end of times. The Cosmos is
vast, and I bring it to life through my imperishable seed,
along with all creatures great and small. Of all the
living variety in the universe that issues forth from
wombs, I am the Holy Father. Just as this is so, the
Cosmos issues forth the sources of delusion: Light,
Darkness, and the Chaos in between. These are the very
chains that bind mankind to slavery, for they are pairs
of opposites I have warned you of already. Even the
shining Light can be a delusion. While its purest form
can reveal even the Soul, it can blind you and cause you
to long for the lesser lights of worldly happiness and
transient knowledge. Chaos is its own pair of opposites,
being merely one's inability to distinguish between
Light and Dark. It will cause you to be ruled by unruly
passions, with insatiable thirst for pleasure and
possessions. Chaos will bind you to restlessness without
end. Darkness, as you may have guessed, is the chain
that binds through ignorance, confusion, laziness, and
indecision. While the Light enslaves the happy, and
Chaos binds the ambitious, Darkness is the shackle of
the ignorant.

"These forces take turns rising in the minds of people, confusing them in waves. For example, when you feel the onset of sudden understanding, know that Light prevails. When you feel the bloodlust in the heat of battle, or greed, or impatience, know that Chaos dominates. When you are feeling dull, confused, not knowing which way to turn – know that Darkness prevails at that time. If you live your life in Light, you will have Light everlasting upon death. If you live in Chaos, you will be resurrected into the bonds of action once again. If you live in Darkness, resurrection only begets more Darkness for you. Those who sew righteousness in their actions will reap Light, with joy unspeakable and full of glory! The seeds of Chaos grow only pain. Planting in Darkness will surely only bring ignorance in the fall. Light leads to knowledge. Chaos leads to greed. Darkness leads to confusion and stupidity. If you live in the Light, you rise to heaven. If you dwell in Chaos, you remain chained to Earthly desires. Darkness, your lowest nature, is its own hell.

"The wise know that these Three Delusions are the real motivations behind every action. The wise also understand that knowing what is beyond them leads to union with Me. When the Soul has overcome the Delusions that are the cause of the body, itself, that person shall not perish, but have everlasting life. Such a person is said to have transcended the Delusions, having neither love for Light, Chaos, or Darkness when they dominate, nor longing for them when they cease. Stoic, this person is undisturbed by Delusion, knowing it to be the motive behind all action, still armed with the sword of gnosis. The inner peace of the Soul is where this person resides, experiencing happiness and suffering as the same thing. This person sees gold, mud, and stone of equal value. Both blame and praise are of no interest. Neither honor nor insult provokes an outburst. Much like you, while in battle this person sees no side as his enemy or ally. There is never felt a lack of anything, so therefore no need for action. This is true gnosis!

"Whoever believeth in Me with unwavering love will rise above Delusion, dwelling with me as One forever and ever. For I am the Lord, thy God – the eternal Soul within the body. I shall never die. I am the Way, the Truth, and the Life – joy eternal forever and ever."

The Lord Most High

"You probably know the ancient story of the Tree of Knowledge," Chris continued. "The tree is eternal, with its roots in heaven and its branches stretching towards the Cosmos. On each of its leaves is written a verse, and whoever knows the Tree knows all holy books. The great arcs of the branches are fed by the Delusions, and the buds that grow from them are all the objects of the senses. Its roots are the roots of all human action. Its full form, from top to bottom and all its girth, can never be fully comprehended. Therefore, one must sharpen one's skills of indifference to these sense objects as one would sharpen an axe to cut down the Tree. Once this Tree of Pairs of Opposites is cut through, people can enter a garden from which no death shall remove them. They will dwell with the Eternal Creator, the wellspring from which all of this apparent activity flows without end. When these people have finally thrown off the manacles of pride and ignorance, they are free from Delusion. This is the conquest of attachment to worldly things! Their Souls then exist in eternal union with God. Without want, they no longer are the slaves constrained only to reflexive reaction to pairs of opposites appearing before them. Then they will have reached a state of peace.

"This is the nature of my Infinite Self. Neither the sun, nor the moon, nor any fire you may imagine can shine upon Me, for I am Light Eternal, and whosoever shall reach me will never die. Those three Lesser Lights take their luminescence from Me! My energy flows through the sun and sustains all life there. As the moon, I move the tides and give the cycles to the plants and trees with their sap. My flame is the combustion of all foods within all beings, turning them into energy and strengthening the body. Part of Me is the God within every creature that lives. This is the eternal nature of the Soul, appearing as a separate thing that puts on the material of mind, body, and the senses as one would put on clothes. When the Lord wears a material body, or tosses it aside, it is Him entering or departing the World. When He leaves, in death, He takes the mind and senses with him as surely as the wind carries away the scent of a flower. While in life, though, He sits behind the senses, a witness and guardian, enjoying and suffering throughout. In His mortal form, living and dying, He knows even the inner moods and subtle emotions. The ignorant can never see Him thus, but the saints and sages see him with their wisdom. The gnostic who has reached discernment and disinterest through the various spiritual practices will see Him inside themselves. Others may never find Him, lost in their desire to do just that. Nonetheless, He is in all hearts! He giveth and taketh away memory, thoughts, and knowledge. He is all that the scriptures teach. He is the Teacher. He is the Knower.

"Now, the most sacred of all truths: It is thought that there exists only two kinds of beings – the mortal beings and the immortal beings. God is immortal and eternal. The nature of all creatures, to include mankind, is mortal. But, there is one more kind – the Enlightened Being, also called One. The One is the Spirit that pervades the Cosmos. Since I transcend both the mortal and the immortal, I am known to these Beings and in the holy texts as the Ultimate Reality. Knowing me as the Ultimate Reality means knowing all that can be known. Those who know me thus do so by freeing themselves from Delusion and adoring Me wholeheartedly. This knowledge is true wisdom, and the fulfillment of life's purpose."

On the Divine and Demonic Tendencies of Mankind

"Those who are born with divine disposition often exhibit fearlessness – blessed are these who are pure in heart. Following the scriptures and the lessons therein, such a person overcomes all obstacles in the path to union with God. This person is in control of the passions, is charitable, honest, and of even temper – doing no harm to others. People so disposed are compassionate, without greed, renouncing worldly possessions with a calm mind and soothing tongue. Gentle and modest, they engage only in useful activities with faith in the strength of their divine nature. Enduring all and forgiving all, these people are of pure thoughts and pure actions. They abandon hatred and pride. These qualities are innate, and lead to liberation. Fear not, A.J., for it is obvious by your inner conflict that you are of divine nature – for it is said that some people are more conscientious than others, and they are the ones who will suffer.

"However, some people are born with demonic tendencies, and their innate characteristics are arrogance, hypocrisy, anger, willful ignorance, and cruelty. These unfortunate people, beyond merely the godless who do not believe in the scriptures, believe the universe to be unbound by *any* moral law. Believing the animal laws of reproduction and survival are the only cause and reason for existence, at the expense of all other laws, they seek to destroy their own worlds through atrocities– the enemies of civilization. Such people possess desires that can never be satiated, driving headlong towards fruits unclean and evil without even knowing. Self-interested, vain, arrogant, and prideful, they believe without a doubt that the meaning of life is gratification. They strive endlessly, dishonestly, to amass the wealth they need to slake their unending thirst. So, these people become chained to their every want, every worry, every longing, until death is the only release. They say to everyone 'Look! I bought this thing I wanted today. Tomorrow I'll want something else and have to go get it. Look at how much money I have! I'll have even more soon. I've beaten everyone who's come against me, and I'll beat anyone else who challenges my dominance. I'm the boss! Look at all my stuff, my success, my strength – look how happy I am! Nobody is as awesome as I am. I have money, and come from a good family, so I'll just go to church, tithe, pray to God, and then do whatever I like.' These people are the truly Godless – the true unbelievers.

"Addicted to whatever will bring them sensual gratification, the demonic are driven relentlessly by desire, and thus Delusion. They are trapped in the hell of their own minds. Overconfident, condescending, self-aggrandizing, and drunk on money, they make their religion a show. They do not understand their own sacred rituals. Truly, they are the ones who hate Me by denying that their Souls and those of others are all Me. They are my enemies, and time and again I deny them the Kingdom of God and cast them back into the world of birth and death. Rather than being reborn unto Me, the demonic are reborn into Delusion anew. Farthest from my presence, they are the most troubled.

"The three doors to hell are lust, rage, and greed. Any one of these, unchecked, can lead to a person's downfall. Avoid these evil doors! Passing them by leads to salvation – the highest goal. Those who ignore what I have taught, acting instead on impulse and desire alone, will not reach this goal. Therefore, let my teachings be your guide, A.J., so that you can decide what actions to take and what actions to avoid. To act, learn the Path of Action as I have taught and then act accordingly."

The Three Kinds of Faith

A.J. thought about what he had just heard, and how almost everyone he knows back home might fit into the category of 'demonic'. He knew many people who sought out only the best things, amassed money and belongings, advocated torture and war, dismissed the poor as 'lazy', and counted their fortunes of wealth and health as 'blessings' every Sunday in church, if they even went. He asked Chris about this state of things back home. "I see a lot of people who pray to God with a lot of love and faith in their hearts, but they don't seem to actually *do* the things that are taught to them in scripture. You said these people are in Delusion. What kind of Delusion is this faith? Is it Light, Dark, or Chaotic?"

"A.J.," Chris began, "you have observed astutely. Therefore, I will tell you there are three kinds of faith among human beings, each corresponding to either Light, Darkness, or Chaos. As you may expect, people whose spirit is dominated by Light will worship God truly, even in His various forms. People of Chaos only truly worship wealth and power. Those who have a proclivity towards Darkness worship the dead, thinking that all manner of ghosts, ancestors, and spirits are gods. Many of these people are of the Demonic type, bound to the objects of this world by lust and vanity. They may even go so far as to mortify their flesh through drugs or abuse in an effort to weaken the grasp of their senses on reality. Since I am the one who dwells within, this outrages me!

"All aspects of worship may be used to distinguish between the three types of churchgoers. You could look at how they pray, for example, or maybe in what they abstain from, or in how they give to charity. Let me draw a parallel with food, in these cases, so that you may understand. If you look at the worship practices of people influenced by Light, as if it were food, it would be vital, energizing, strengthening, and healthy. This food gives not only physical pleasure, but mental sharpness and enjoyment – juicy and fresh, healing and good. The Chaotic, however, prefer worship that, as a food, is extremely bitter, or outrageously hot, or salty, sour, acidic – whatever is punishing. Such foods may even be unhealthy, or at least disruptive to the body and senses. The Dark, in their worship, have a perverse taste for the tasteless, a love for the rotten, and an inclination to the impure. They especially love food from the plates of others.

"You see, A.J., when worship is performed rightly, without any desire for advantage to one's self, this is of the Light. The prayers are offered, thus, for their own sake. The worshiper is motivated only by duty. Rest assured, though, that worship done either for outward show or for the hope of divine reward in the hereafter is motivated by Chaos. Those inspired by Darkness don't even care if the worship is done properly, whether it be an offering, or prayer, or tithing – no faith at all!

"Worshiping in the Light is a threefold path, itself. It is comprised of three kinds of self-control. The first, self-control of the body, involves reverence for the angels and the saints, respect for the teachers, doing no harm, straight dealings with others, physical hygiene, and temperance of one's sexual desires. Self-control of the speech is the second, requiring one to speak without hurting others, without lying, while striving to benefit others in kindness and to study My teachings. Self-control of the mind will be familiar to you as meditation upon the Soul, requiring sympathy, serenity, integrity, and the detachment of the senses from the objects of their desire. This is enlightened faith. However, there are those who practice self-control under the auspices of Chaos, seeking to gain fame and followers by their feats of austerity. For them, the benefits will be transient because, as it is said, expectation may end in fruition. Those who worship in Darkness may pray or perform rituals with the aim to harm others. Often, they practice the austerity of self-torture for the sake of its excitement, or even turn self-control outward as the control and harm of others.

"Even outside of formal worship, all acts of faith fall within these three categories. For example, even the giving of a gift is subject to the motives of the giver. Gifts given to a deserving person at an appropriate occasion, without regard for past or future benefits from the recipient, is done in the Light. This person gives only because it is the right thing to do. Bound by the greed that arises from Chaos, some give with the hope

of reciprocity, or reward even in the hereafter. They
might even give reluctantly, with an eye towards their
own loss. Darkness reigns when a gift is given to
someone undeserving, or given inappropriately. These
gifts are given either without regard for the feelings of
the recipient, or to intentionally harm them. You see, all
the saints, all the scriptures, and all the sacred rituals
were created by God in ancient times through Faith,
Hope, and Charity. Therefore, Faith is the watchword of
all who are about to undertake any act of worship,
prayer, or giving. Hope is the goodness, the
perseverance, and the dedication in the heart of these
worshipers. Charity is eternal, extending beyond the
grave, and is the motive of the liberated who desire no
reward for their worship. Outside of these, without the
faith and will directed only towards God, no sacrifice,
no gift, and no prayer will produce any real effect either
in this world or the hereafter."

The Path of Salvation

As A.J. listened to Chris's words, he remembered himself passing from Darkness to Light in his own life, throwing off the hateful and selfish ways of his youth and joining the Army after 9-11. A pacifist before, his only thought was to protect those he loved – his first act of selflessness and of true devotion. He had liberated himself from selfish intent at that moment, and became free from attachment to even his mortal life. He still wondered, however, what the exact difference was between 'liberation' and 'freedom from attachment'. The concepts seemed similar. He asked Chris.

"A.J.," Chris said, "I want you to know the truth about this difference. The saints have said that 'liberation' means the complete abandonment of actions that have their motives in desire. They say that 'non-attachment' means not desiring the fruits of your actions. Some mystics say that all action should be abandoned, because they believe any action contains at least some evil. Yet other thinkers say that actions of worship, such as prayer and tithing, should not be abandoned. The truth is that these thinkers are correct, because the acts of worship, rightly done, can be purifying to those who understand their true nature. Even so, such worship must be done without hope for the fruits thereof – such is my Will and Judgement.

"There are three kinds of liberation, corresponding to the three Delusions of course. When a person performs an action that does not violate My teachings, and does it only because of duty and without hope for reward or reciprocation, this action is done in the Light. Of course, avoiding an action due to fear that it might be painful, or unpleasant, is done under the influence of Chaos. If a person simply shirks duty and forsakes those actions which are necessary, this is Darkness. However, people like you, A.J., are gifted with gnosis, and illuminated by the true knowledge of the Soul! You should have no doubt about it. You do not shrink from your duty simply because you find it disagreeable at the moment. Likewise, you do not seek out comfort for yourself before your subordinates. It would be inconceivable that a human being could give up *all* action and do nothing! Giving up the fruits of those actions, on the other hand, is true non-attachment. Those who are not like you, who have not overcome the ego and its lust, will surely experience the fruits of their actions. Some will be sweet, yes. Some will be bitter, of course. Some will just be somewhere in between. Whether or not they are pleasant may not even have any relationship to the original action — reaped only as they ripen. Those with gnosis will harvest no such fruit either in this world or in the hereafter.

"Listen and I teach you now the wisdom that will break the bondage of your deeds. Those with little or no gnosis are under the illusion that the Soul is the driving force behind actions. These people have not yet worked to rid their minds of Delusion. The real impulse to act comes from the mortal body itself, the ego, the senses, the machinations of the organs, and the angels looking over it all in spirit. No matter what one does, thinks, or says, whether it be good or evil, this is always the case. If one's mind is beyond attachment, however, and not controlled by the ego – there is no deed that can bind that person with any chain." Chris looked out over the darkness and stretched an arm towards the Iraqi lines. "Though you may kill a thousand of these men, A.J.," he said, "you are no murderer.

"I'll tell you more. We already talked about Knowledge, the Knower, and That which is Known – all motivating action. Yet there are three components even to action. All action has an Instrument, a Purpose, and a Doer of the action. Looking just at Knowledge, Action, and Doer from among these, it is said that these each have three types according to which Delusion dominates them at a given time. First, let me teach you about Knowledge, in this sense. There is Knowledge in Light, which recognizes Cosmos - everything, even the eternal Souls of every single creature, are one single being. Knowledge in Chaos, however, only sees the divisions between the beings – existence as separate objects and things. Knowledge in Darkness sees only a distorted version of nature, without reason, and mistaking the small part that can be known for all that is. Now about Action: In the Light, Action is done for the sake of duty alone, and without desire for the fruits of the undertaking. Action in Light is done without desire, care, or compulsion. Action in Chaos is driven by lust and ego as twin masters, cracking the whip, flying in the face of Nature. In Darkness, Action flows from ignorance without regard to consequences, wasting resources in the process. Dark Action, overconfident and without introspection, careless of who it harms, is undertaken brashly. As for the Doer of these Actions, you can recognize one walking in the Light because that person is unfazed by both victory and loss, being without desire for either – neither bemoaning the unfairness of a failure nor bragging upon triumph. With crass desire, however, jumping at the chance to flaunt success, one is said to be a Doer in Chaos. Such people will pursue their aims ruthlessly, blaming others for their failures. In Darkness, the Doer is altogether indifferent to the task - cheating, cutting corners, dithering, acting easily hurt, and doing whatever is possible to avoid work.

"Along with what I have just told you, human beings possess three kinds of Conscience. Conscience in the Light can be noticed in one who can see what path leads to Liberation, and what path leads to mere desire for worldly things. With this power, such a person can simply know right from wrong, good from evil, and what should and should not be done. This person can clearly see which choices will enslave, and which will set free. Of course, when the Conscience cannot differentiate between these concepts, in confusion, this is Chaos at work again. Conscience in Darkness, in its sheer ignorance, mistakes wrong for right, good for evil, or else doesn't care which is which.

"Human kind also carries with it three kinds of Will. When inspired by Light, divine, the Will is unwavering. One who energetically practices gnosis with an aim to refine the mind and senses can strengthen even this kind of determined Will. In Chaos, of course, the Will is a force driving for reward or personal gain, doing one thing after another with an eye always focused on the objects of desire. The Dark Will is mere stubbornness, even in spiritual matters where there is simply an obstinate refusal to leave behind vanity, self-pity, fear, hate, and willful ignorance.

"There exist, also, three kinds of Joy in this world. The highest of these is the Joy found in the truth of Light. One who knows the Soul as God knows this Joy. This kind of righteous knowledge comes only through one's own hard work and introspection. Difficult at first, the labor leads to suffering's end. Chaos, too, contains a kind of joy, but it is of the fleeting and impermanent kind. It is the Joy of a new purchase, or a desire fulfilled, but it will fade in time and more want will fill the void. Avoid this temptation as you would a poisoned chalice. Joy found in Darkness, and it is there to be found, is often masochistic, sadistic, but can take the lesser forms of idle contentment or sloth. The period of this Joy is an illusion, though.

"There are no beings on heaven or Earth, neither mortal nor angel, who are entirely free from influence of the three Delusions that emanate from the Cosmos. The arc of everyone's life, whether sage or seeker, master or servant, is at least initially described by these Delusions. This is what people these days mistakenly call 'karma', but that is not correct. The direction one's life moves is not a matter of some simple system of 'good' and 'bad' points whereby one's fortunes are determined. Rather, one's life is initially propelled along a path determined by the Delusions into which one is born, continuing along this path without deviation unless acted on by an outside force. For example, the path of the sage is foreordained – to be calm of mind and steady of Spirit, upright, forgiving, stoic, and without blemish. This person seeks wisdom, seeks to know the Soul, and has firm faith in God. A leader, on the other hand, is set to the path of fearlessness, boldness, generosity, and mastery of skills. A combat leader, in particular, has a proclivity for bravery and an appetite for decisive action in battle. This setting of initial conditions is the same for businesspeople, farmers, public servants, or whomever. For each, their work is set before them as a duty. Thus, mankind is born to be perfect, and every person can attain that perfection through recognizing the path, the trajectory, and working accordingly.

"Let me explain in more detail, A.J., how devotion to one's work can lead to perfection. As I have mentioned before, a person who works without anxiety for results or hope for its fruits will be free from bondage. Indeed, the performance of one's duty entirely as an act of worship to the Lord is the straight path to perfection. This is because He is the source of all action and all work everywhere and always, and such labor will bring the seeker into direct union with Him. So long as the work being done is aligned with one's natural path and predisposition, even if not perfectly done, it is work without sin. Work done otherwise, even if done well, is by its very nature contrived to achieve some material goal and should be avoided. Just as an object in motion tends to remain on its path unless disturbed, a person's path *can* be altered. This is certain. However, the object also tends to resist too much change given to it too quickly. This can lead to perturbation, so it is better to make incremental changes. Work that is done imperfectly but true to one's nature should be pursued without discouragement because nothing within the Cosmos is perfect. It's as natural as the smoke from any fire – the result of incomplete combustion.

"Listen, what I'm telling you about work is the very definition of freedom from attachment. Through gnosis, freedom from desire and attachment leads to union with God, whose throne is beyond all work and action. Such a person is One with God, the objective and goal of all wisdom. This is achieved by all the things I have taught you up to this point: taming of the senses through resolute application of the Will, throwing overboard attachment to the alternate delights and terrors of sight, sound, and tastes of this world, without lust and without fear for either. Thus, A.J., seek peaceful surroundings, be comfortable alone with your own thoughts, avoid gluttony, and be modest of speech. Engage your whole person in contemplation of God's true nature. Be compassionate, and do away with violence, pride, lust, vanity, anger, and love of your possessions. Free yourself from your sense of self-importance and calm your heart and mind. Don't grieve so deeply, and don't crave so greatly. See all people as created equal. In your mind, know that I am the true doer of all action. Thus, love Me as you would love a family member – your life's stronghold in times of siege.

"Keep your heart and mind united with Me and My grace will carry you through any battle. However if you ignore Me, in your arrogance you toss aside what I have told you this night - you are lost to Me. If in self-pity you say 'I will not fight,' then you take My words in vain. Have you learned nothing! Your own actions leading to this night have created the path you now travel – the arc of your life leads here without straying! Even though you ignorantly seek to avoid fighting the enemy, your own nature will drive you to do it! You are powerless to move the object from its path at this late hour. But take heart, A.J., and fear not, for I am alive in the hearts of every living thing. It is my Will that drives the endless cycles of life. Use what I have taught you, and your own gnosis, to take refuge in me only. If you do all this, you love Me most dearly. You can know My truth and My deepest nature by loving Me. That knowledge leads to immediate union with Me. All you do will be as a sacred offering to Me, given without evasion, and My grace will be upon you. You will find eternal peace.

"Think deeply on what I have just given you, for it is the holiest of holies – the ineffable and lost secret. I give it to you, A.J., for your own benefit. You are a friend of God, so adore Me with your whole heart as I have chosen to love you. Always worship Me, and have no other gods. Do these things, kneeling to Me alone, and you will find Me – this is My covenant. Perform your duties within Me and see Me as your refuge and your strength. Have no fear for I will free you from bondage and keep you from sin.

"A final caution, A.J.: You must never reveal any of the secret arts, parts, or points of this holy truth to anyone who lacks self-discipline and commitment, or who hate's his or her teacher and mocks Me. However, those who love me, and teach this ultimate truth of God to My believers, will dwell with Me forever. Such are my disciples who are dearer to Me than anyone on Earth, for they do Me the highest service. Such others who study what we have discussed here tonight will be considered to have worshiped Me in spirit. Even those who merely hear the words faithfully spoken and believed will be considered by Me to be righteous, spared from sin and lifted to Heaven.

The Path of Mysticism

"A.J.," Chris continued, "since you seem to already know and accept Me, I think I will tell you the innermost secret. It is the Truth within the sanctum sanctorum- the knowledge of God. This is not knowledge that can be had through reason. It is nearer than that. It can be had through clear vision, instantly and directly. If you can understand this you will be free forever. This kind of knowledge is above all other kinds. It is the kind only the mystics can know. It is powerful knowledge, but easily had. Through it, one can be brought to the Eternal Truth. Those who are without faith, in Me or in my knowledge, will fail to find Me in this way. They will have to turn back and strengthen their gnosis through yet another birth and death of the self.

"Every crevice of the Universe is pervaded by Me in My form that is eternal and unknowable to the senses. All living things exist within Me, though I cannot be said to exist within them. You must understand that they do not physically exist within me, I being a mere container. This is My divine mystery that you must try to understand. My very being *sustains* all creatures and brings them into being, yet has no physical interaction with them in the worldly sense. All things wander freely within me in this way. And as the cosmic sunset of the ages approaches, I gather them back unto Me. When the sunrise breaks, so too I bring them into being again. All are powerless against my Word and my Will, for I created this illusion that is their master, and I am the Master of the Illusion, the King of Secrets. Forever and always I issue the multitudes of lives forth from My being.

"Though all are bound by these acts, I stand apart, indifferent, unbound to the results, watching over the illusion, the Creator. The illusory nature of the world is the very thing that allows all other things to come into being, to move, and to remain. Dear A.J., that is why the many worlds spin, and ours is filled with its birth and destruction! Fools who know me in only my human form know nothing at all of Me, who is the Lord of their soul! All of their hopes, their labors, and their knowledge is in vain. They are fooled by their own supposed understanding. They exist in a state of madness, like psychopaths and monsters.

"The souls of those who become godlike, who know Me as the Alpha, without end, are great. They offer Me devotion and an unwavering mind. They praise My strength in word and in deed for all times, striving to be virtuous so that they can find Me. Unwavering in their promises to themselves, worshipful, they are always unified with Me. Some others may at least know that I am in all things, sometimes seeing themselves as part of the Universe and sometimes separate from it. There are even others who simply worship from among the countless numbers of gods and goddesses – these are simply my many faces. I am these gods, and the rituals prescribed by their many religions. I am also the offerings made to spirits of the dead, and the healing foods of the Earth. I am the many names of God, and the ineffable ones. Not only am I the sacrifice, and the flame, but the offering itself! I am the Father and Mother, the granter of rewards, the purifier. I am Absolute Knowledge. I am every book of scripture of every religion. I am the Lord at the final destination, the Giver of Life. Not only am I at the end, but at the beginning as well, and every place of dwelling between. I am friend and salvation to all. I am Death and Heaven, the eternal germ within all living things. I am the sun, the fire, the heat of both, the rain, the drought, and the cause of both. I am all of the known Universe, and all of the unknown Universe.

"Many men and women are versed in scripture, worshiping Me, taking communion, and confessing their sins. These people pray for Heaven, on Earth and at death. Achieving this they soon find that they are never released from the mortal world of desire- even for the desire of Heaven's peace and delights. This is the path of those who call themselves righteous. But some, even worshiping the various deities scattered through the many religions, have true faith in their hearts and an undistracted mind. These people are really worshiping Me, and I will look over them. Even so, these worshipers will make several returns to and rebirths from the mortal world before knowing Me in my true form. The worshipers of the various gods will come to know only those gods, just as the worshipers of ancestors' spirits will only know those spirits. The worshipers of the elements, too, will know only those elements. Likewise, those who worship Me will come to Me.

"To worship me takes no elaborate sacrifice. Whatever is offered in true devotion, a flower or even a petal, is the gift of love. Whatever ritual, whatever gift given to another person, whatever promise of spiritual improvement- all can be truly devoted to Me. Doing so relieves one from both the good and the evil fruits of the devotion. These are devotions done for the sake of devotion, rather than for hopes of salvation. Doing so sets people free from action and inertia, united with Me, even in this life.

"This is the true meaning of morality, and to judge not. To be godlike is to be Me. I see all creation without emotion- without hating or loving anything. Even so, all people are within Me always, and I can be seen within them, shining forth from them. Even those who are stained by sins need only to love Me in complete devotion and all will be washed away. To me, I see none of those sins and those people are as holy as any part of the Universe is holy. This holiness will, eventually, transform the sinners and give them eternal peace. Those who love Me shall not perish, but have peace everlasting. Even people who believe themselves to be lowly can reach this highest place just as those high-priests, kings, and philosophers can, simply by taking refuge in me.

"A.J., you are living in the transient world of the
deceiving senses, without joy. Simply turn your
attention towards Me instead, and come into my Being."

Glory of the Divine

"Great Warrior," Chris addressed A.J. now in a booming, triumphant voice, "I can see that your heart deeply enjoys My Word, the highest wisdom. So, I will tell you that even the saints and angels cannot know My origins. I AM the origin, the giver of life to the saints and angels. Only those who know the birthless and deathless nature of the Lord of the Worlds are without sin, untroubled by delusion. Consider all that makes a person great: knowledge, power, clarity, truth, calmness, discipline, forbearance, happiness, sorrow, birth and death- I am the source of all these. I am that which fears, and that which is fearless, harming no creature. A person's unshaken mind, happy heart, stark will, giving hand, fame, honor, and even infamy- all given by My Word. It is from my Mind alone that the sages, the saints, and all ancestors and founders of all the peoples were born.

"Those who can grasp the infinite complexity of my Being, present everywhere and for all times, live within my Knowledge. I am the Alpha, and the source of life that the wise can see when they worship with hearts full of love. When they do, the mind and senses are absorbed in Me as the single focus of their prayers. The mind and the senses reveal to each other Heaven. In this way, the devoted are always aware of their Lord. Awareness illuminates the thoughts of the worshipers, guiding them towards Me always. I even exist in the

hearts of the ignorant, through My own Grace and
Mercy, in the form of Knowledge- the lamp that shines
its Light in the darkness."

Having been brought from darkness to light by
Chris's words, and in a state of profound awe, A.J.'s
voice rose in praise, "You are God the Highest, and
utterly holy! You are the One talked about by the true
saints, Lord of the Angels. I've heard it before from
others but now I hear it directly from you! What you
tell me is the Truth! I know it in my heart! You are the
King of Kings, Lord of the World, the source of all
things. How could angels or giants even know your
Glory entirely? Only you can know this absolute Truth,
because you are what you are. Because you are these
things, you have the power to make me know your true
form! Show me your real nature, how you appear to
those who pray and meditate, what you really are
behind the manifestations and illusions that I have seen
until now. Tell me all of your powers in Heaven and on
Earth! You could speak forever and I would never get
tired!"

Chris, again soothing and reassuring, spoke,
"My dear A.J., I will certainly tell you of my many
forms, but I will limit it to the main ones. Of the lesser
forms, there is an infinite number. Know this, though,
that I am the Immortal Soul that lives in the hearts of
all people. I am Birth and Death. I am all of the gods of
the sun, the moon, and the wind. I am the King of
Heaven. I am the mind that rules the senses, and the
consciousness in the living. I am all gods and all things.

I am the Alpha and the Omega, and all of Creation
between. I am Spiritual Knowledge, and the Logic in all
argument. I am Infinite Time, everywhere and in all
things. I am the Reaper, and the Mother. I am the
melody of music, and the rhythm of poetry. I am the
skill of the skilled, the strength of the strong, and the
purity of the good. I am Chris among soldiers, and I am
my friend A.J. among leaders. I am the authority of
rulers, and the thirst of conquerors. I am the silence
within a secret, and the Knowledge of the knower.
These are only a few of my forms, but you don't need to
waste your time with all of this! Simply know that I
exist, and that the Universe is supported by but a single
atom of Myself."

God's True Form Revealed

"Your mystic and sublime words have taught me the truth about the Soul," A.J. said. "I have been moved from ignorance to seeing. By your own grace I have learned the inner mechanism of the birth and death of all living things, and of your own glorious infinity!" Setting aside his nearly overwhelming reverence for the moment, and mustering a new kind of courage never before felt within himself, A.J. made the boldest of requests. "Lord Most High, I do not doubt for an instant that you are exactly as you described yourself – but I must see for myself your true, divine form! If you find me ready and worthy, Lord of Lords, reveal to me your infinite and ultimate being!"

As if by magic, A.J. found himself in the cool night air of the desert. He was outside of the tank, on the other side of the low sand berm they were using for cover. He could see the great tan muzzle of his tank's gun, cold, motionless, hovering inertly just above the mound. He looked up to see Chris standing beside the gun, under the stars and a waxing crescent moon.

Chris spoke. "Alright, my dear friend. Prepare yourself to see what will seem like millions of my divine forms, encompassing every possible permutation of shape, size, and color. But that will only be the beginning, for you will see forms not of this Earth – angels, demons, gods of other worlds – the likes of which have never before been conceived in the minds of men, let alone actually seen by humans. Indeed, you will see all things in the universe, living and otherwise, contained within my single body. You will see everything you have ever imagined, and everything you have never imagined. You won't be able to see any of this, however, with those human eyes. Behold!"

Chris laid his hands upon A.J. "I give you the power of divine sight!"

With those words A.J. was immersed in a vision that was beyond mere words. The transcendent, divine form of the Lord contained not just the many, but the ALL! All mouths, all eyes, all shapes and forms that existed everywhere and at all times throughout the universe, its past, and its future. A.J. witnessed heavenly objects he could not describe and alien notions he could not comprehend – weapons, ornaments, clothes, scents, sensations, emotions, revelations of Truth, ideas – splendid, terrible, without bounds, for ever and ever. The grandeur of the moment was as bright as a thousand nuclear blasts, but not unpleasant or painful. The entire universe in its full scale and scope, but also stretching in dimensions A.J. had never know before, was laid out before him to be comprehended as a single entity. The very edges, the very centers, all that is seen, all that is occulted, all that ever was, and all that ever will be – all of this was his as a single gulp of air. The profane and the divine were One.

Then A.J., overawed by the gift of divine sight, crumpled to the sand in a heap at Chris's feet. The hair stood on the back of his neck in a chill as he fully grasped whose presence he was in. "Oh Lord," he gasped, "I can see all the other gods within you arranged according to your plan! I can see every creature on every planet, strange and wonderful! I see all of the imagined forms of the Creator seated on their thrones, yet within you! I see all the saints and serpents. I see the universe eternal, infinite in its parts, without end, middle, or beginning in time. Crowned in unimaginable glory, you wield the most powerful of symbols, shining and brilliant as an infinite sun! I can plainly see you are the sum of all knowledge, the immovable cornerstone and unshakable temple, the undying soul within and guardian beyond the eternal law. Without birth or death, you are the ultimate strength in the universe, and the destroyer of worlds. You are the four winds, the eternal sky, the span between heaven and Earth. Your terrible and mighty form shakes every plane of existence! The saints and demigods enter into you in prayer and supplication, trembling in fear. The prophets and the seers sing your praises of peace and adoration. All of the gods, demigods, demons, and angels look upon your true form in amazement and awe – struck with fear and astonishment at your vast complexity and beauty as I am even now!

"But your brilliance is at the same time frightful. When I see that you are everywhere, supporting the

very sky as a rainbow, your terrible power at your
fingertips, peace leaves me and I am frightened! Even as
you contain all the good in the world, I also see you
create the fires of Doomsday. I become so confused I
don't know which way is up, for I see all the soldiers of
our army, and of my enemy, and millions of others,
kings, the distinguished and revered, rushing into your
jaws to be crushed to bits and destroyed! Like moths to
the flame, I see the hosts of all men from all times,
heroes and warriors, flow into your destructive fires like
rivers flow into the ocean. I can see in you the
destruction of entire worlds by tongues of fire and rays
of unimaginably powerful energy from space! These
scenes trouble me so. Have mercy and make me
understand who you are and have always been!"

Chris's voice now boomed in A.J.'s head, "I am
Time, the reaper of all people, as grain that ripens to the
inevitable harvest. This army of your enemies before
you must all die, and your army, and all others. Fight,
don't fight – it doesn't matter. Since it doesn't, it is then
better for a warrior to fight! Achieve glory, and
promotion, and awards for yourself. Get up, A.J., you
professional soldier and master of your trade! You will
only seem to kill, but by my Will these men are already
slain. You only shoot the dead, doomed already to their
heroic ends. Have not fear, for the enemy is yours!"

A.J. heard and understood these words,
gathering himself even in his fear, but remaining
prostrate at Chris's feet in profound awe. His voice still
trembling, but now from the all-consuming gravity of

the moment rather than raw terror, he said, "I see now
the good that is the world according to your Will. Even
demons flee in panic and terror at your sight, and the
angels bow their heads and avert their eyes at your
presence. How could they dare to do otherwise? After
all, you are the Prime Mover of all, even of people's
conception of the Creator – eternal, Lord of Hosts,
sustainer of the world. You are all that is and all that is
not – and all that transcends both! You are the King of
Heaven, the most ancient. The entire cosmos sits
securely within your Will. You are the knowledge of all
that thinks, the goal of all struggles, eternal change, and
the entirety of creation. You are the Lord of Death,
Lord of the Cosmos and all its heavenly bodies, and all
that composes the Earth. You are the Father of Fathers,
and of all who are born. All praise belongs to you, from
all corners of creation. Infinite and boundless, you must
be all that there is since you are seen everywhere and in
all things."

A.J. stopped in thought as he suddenly
remembered how casually, and sometimes crassly, he
had addressed his friend up until this night. "Without
knowing, I've been calling you 'Chris' and 'brother',
mistaking the undying for mere mortality. My mere
brotherly love could never have been worthy of your
true greatness. I remember I would joke and mess
around in front of you in the chow hall, or in formation,
or back in the barracks. I had no idea! Did I offend?
Please forgive me! I had no way of knowing you were
the architect of the universe, moved by nothing yet the

power of all that moves. The seven heavens contain no higher being, none more worthy of worship." A.J. threw himself even lower to the ground in shame. "Forgive me," he begged "as a Father to a son, as would one soldier to another, or as anyone to their closest companion! I have seen what has been hidden from all other men and I am thankful, but your true form is too much for me to bear!"

Chris's voice was kind, as a parent to a child scared of the dark. "This is my form: the primeval and all-pervasive energy of the Cosmos. By my own power I was able to show you, A.J., among all men, and make you see my Divine Light. I showed you because I love you. There is no amount of prayer, or sacrifice, or recitation of scripture, or tithing, or fasting, or any other ritual that will lead anyone else to see me in this way, O Leader of Men. But fear no more! I'll change back to how you first knew me."

With that, Chris returned to his original, human form under the desert moon. A.J. was instantly relieved and regained his feet. Strangely, and as if awakened only a moment ago, the details of Chris's true form began to slip from his mind as a dream. As if reading his thoughts, Chris continued, "My true form is difficult to comprehend, isn't it? Even the angels never see it. Remember what I said about no amount of prayer or ritual can reveal it – only through intense and single-minded devotion can that form be seen, understood, and entered into, O Warrior of Warriors. It is only those people who drive towards me alone, with no attachment

of the senses and free from hatred towards anything
that lives, who will know me."

The Path of Devotion

As the terrible and beautiful image passed slowly from A.J.'s mind, he thought about what Chris had just said. It occurred to him, and he asked out loud, "Some worship God simply through unwavering love, and others by contemplating His omnipotent and eternal being. Which kind of worshiper has a better understanding of devotion?"

Chris, now standing before A.J. in an olive green tanker's coverall, began to explain. "The worshipers who are fixed on me with love in their hearts and an unwavering faith have a greater understanding of devotion. However, the ones who worship my eternal, omnipotent, omnipresent, ineffable, and changeless nature possess great faculties of self-control and restraint of the wandering senses. Their tranquil minds see plainly the soul of every living thing, and are devoted to the welfare of all humanity. These others, too, will come to know me, but it is just a harder path because the greatness of my true, infinite form is difficult for a finite mind to comprehend. As for the first kind, those who love with unerring faith, they quickly feel my presence by offering me every action and all of their devotion with no other gods before Me. Because of this perfect love, they become bonded to me and will heal their broken hearts and bind up their wounds. Whoever worships me in this way will not perish, but will live within me forever and ever.

"For those who cannot find this path," he went on, "they must try at least to concentrate on me through their daily lives. If they lack the power of concentration, as some naturally do, they must engage in works that will please me. Working for my sake alone will lead to salvation. If such a lifelong commitment is impossible for some, as it often is, then simply surrendering to me is yet another effective path. They can do this by controlling their passions to do evil, and shunning the rewards of every action. Of course, concentration done consciously, with an eye to spiritual improvement, is always better than rote repetition and memorization of ritual and prayer. Even greater is the path that leads to Oneness with Me, but even mere humility and shunning of the fruits of one's labor can bring instant peace to a troubled soul."

Chris put a hand on A.J.'s shoulder and looked him directly in the eye. "Hate no living creature. Be friendly and compassionate to all. Free yourself from the delusion that there is a 'you' that is separate from the Cosmos, and that 'you' possess things. Accept pleasure and pain with equal calmness and indifference. Be forgiving. Be content with yourself. Have self-control. Be constantly joined with Me in prayer. Have unshakeable resolve. Dedicate yourself to Me intellectually and emotionally. Do not disturb your fellow human being. In return, allow nothing of this world to disturb you. Do not be swayed by joy, fear, anxiety, or envy. Be pure and unchained from your animal desires. Be prepared for all things, even the unexpected, so that you are never perturbed. Do not be vain. Do not look forward to the results of your actions. Do not covet what seems pleasing. Do not dread what seems disagreeable. Grieve not over the unpleasant. Remain unfazed by both good and bad luck. Have the same forbearance towards enemies as you would allies. Be humble and unprovoked by insult. Be indifferent to pleasure and pain, heat and cold. Be free from attachment to the material. Receive both praise and blame with equal temperament. Control your speech. Be content with whatever comes your way. Make your home both everywhere and nowhere. Fix your mind on me and fill your heart with devotion. Whoever understands this true wisdom will never die, but have life immortal. They are dear to me."

With this, Chris stepped down from the sand berm behind which A.J.'s tank waited to carry him into battle. He clasped A.J.'s shoulders, raising him to his fullest height. Speaking to his innermost being, Chris asked his beloved friend, "Have you listened carefully to all I have taught you, A.J.? Have I lifted your Delusions?"

A.J., calm of mind and with peace in his heart, was no longer trembling with fear. Knowing his duty, and knowing his Soul, he spoke, "O Lord, by Your grace my Delusions are vanquished. My thoughts are clear. My doubts have vanished. I will do your Will."

Epilogue

Such are the words that fill the heart with Light, the most marvelous dialogue between the great warrior, A.J. Nash, and the Lord Most High. It cannot be heard with earthly ears, but only through the mystery of grace. Thus can be learned the greatest of all building plans from the Grand Architect, Himself! The sacred and wonderful truths the Lord bestowed upon A.J. are a source of eternal rejoicing, as is the true form of God's infinite and eternal Self. It can be assured that wherever A.J. goes, great among armored warriors, the Lord is. There can be found goodness and peace, triumph and glory!

Amen. Peace. Peace. Peace.